American Folklore

THE AMERICAN CHARACTER SERIES
John C. Schweitzer, Consulting Editor

American Folklore

Edited by

PETER POULAKIS

English Department

Decorations by

MARIAN EBERT

CHARLES SCRIBNER'S SONS · NEW YORK

G-12.72[M]

Printed in the United States of America
SBN 684-51545-8
Library of Congress Catalog Card Number 69-10740

Acknowledgments

The editor is indebted to the following authors, publishers, and other
holders of copyright for permission to use copyrighted materials.

Appleton-Century-Crofts for "The Saga of Pecos Bill," by Edward
O'Reilly, in *Century Magazine*, Vol. 106, No. 6 (December 1923) pp.
827–833, copyright 1923 by the Century Company.
Mrs. Henry (Christy MacKaye) Barnes (the Estate of Percy MacKaye)
for "The Cats That Clawed to Heaven," from *Tall Tales of the Kentucky
Mountains*, by Percy MacKaye, Doubleday & Company, Inc., 1926.
The Bobbs-Merrill Company, Inc., Publishers, for "The Return of the
Native," from *Concentrated New England*, by Kenneth L. Roberts, copy-
right 1924 by the Bobbs-Merrill Company, Inc., R 1951 by Kenneth L.
Roberts. For "The Waving of the Spectral Arms," from *From the Hills to
the Sea*, by Archibald Rutledge, copyright © 1958 by the Bobbs-Merrill
Company, Inc.
Mrs. Roark (Mary Rose) Bradford for "The Birth of John Henry," from
John Henry, by Roark Bradford, Harper and Row, Publishers, 1931.

The California Folklore Society for "Grant's Tame Trout," by Samuel T. Farquhar, © 1944 by the California Folklore Society, reprinted from *California Folklore Quarterly* (now *Western Folklore*), III, 177–178.

The *Chicago Tribune* for "Independent Vermonters," from an article by Keith W. Jennison, May 20, 1956, issue of the *Chicago Tribune Magazine*.

Dodd, Mead & Company for "James Bowie to the Rescue," from *Sucker's Progress*, by Herbert Asbury.

Doubleday & Company, Inc., Publishers, for "Brer Fox and the Goobers," from *Stars Fell on Alabama*, by Carl Carmer, copyright 1943 by Carl Carmer. For "Babe Ruth," © 1964 by Paul Gallico, from *The Golden People*, by Paul Gallico; reprinted by permission of Doubleday & Company, Inc.

Helen Hartness Flanders, Springfield, Vermont, for "The Miller's Three Sons" as published in *The New Green Mountain Songster*, Yale University Press © 1939, 1967, p. 11.

Folkways Music Publishers, Inc., New York, N.Y., for "The Frozen Logger," Words and Music by James Stevens, TRO © copyright 1951.

Handy Brothers Music Company, Inc., for "The St. Louis Blues," by W. C. Handy.

Harcourt, Brace & World, Inc., for "Who Made Paul Bunyan?" from *The People Yes*, by Carl Sandburg, copyright 1936 by Harcourt, Brace & World, Inc., renewed 1964 by Carl Sandburg. For "The Lane County Bachelor," from *The American Songbag*, Carl Sandburg, ed., 1927.

Harper & Row, Publishers, for "The Celebrated Jumping Frog of Calaveras County," from *Sketches New and Old*, by Samuel L. Clemens.

Harvard University Press for "The White Stone Canoe" and "Mondawmin or The Origin of Indian Corn," by Henry Rowe Schoolcraft, from *Tales of the North American Indians*, by Flanagan and Hudson.

Holiday House for "The Bedcats," from *Ol' Paul the Mighty Logger*, by Glen Rounds, copyright 1936, 1951.

Holt, Rinehart & Winston, Inc., for "Louis Armstrong on Oliver" from *Hear Me Talkin' to You*, edited by Nat Shapiro and Nat Hentoff, copyright © 1955 by Nat Shapiro and Nat Hentoff. For "Mike Fink and the Kicking Sheriff," from *Mike Fink*, by Walter Blair and Franklin J. Meine. For "The Ballad of William Sycamore" from *Ballads and Poems*, by Stephen Vincent Benét, copyright 1931 by Stephen Vincent Benét, copyright © 1959 by Rosemary Carr Benét. For "The Witch of Coös," from *Complete Poems of Robert Frost*, copyright 1923 by Holt, Rinehart and Winston, Inc., copyright 1951 by Robert Frost.

Messrs Clifford J. Hurston and John C. Hurston for "High John de Conquer" and "How Jack O'Lantern Came to Be," from *Mules and Men*, by Zora Neale Hurston, J. B. Lippincott Company, Publishers.

Alfred A. Knopf, Inc., for "Bras Coupé," from *The French Quarter*, copyright 1936 by Alfred A. Knopf, Inc., and renewed 1964 by Edith Evans Asbury.

J. B. Lippincott Company for "Esau and the Gorbey," from *Ridge Runner, The Story of a Maine Woodsman*, by Gerald Averill, copyright 1948 by J. B. Lippincott Company. For "The Jam on Gerry's Rock," from *The Folklore of Maine*, by Horace P. Beck; copyright © 1957 by Horace P. Beck, published by J. B. Lippincott Company. For "Why Spuyten Duyvil Is So Named," from *Myths and Legends of Our Own Land*, by Charles M. Skinner (Vol. I, pp. 51–52).

Ludlow Music, Inc., for "The Buffalo Skinners," from *Cowboy Songs and Other Frontier Ballads* (pp. 158–161), Collected, Adapted and Arranged by John A. Lomax and Alan Lomax © copyright 1934 and renewed 1962 Ludlow Music., Inc., New York, N.Y.

David McKay Company for "The Lavender Evening Dress" from *Dark Trees to the Wind*, by Carl Carmer, copyright 1949 by Carl Carmer. For "Louis Armstrong on the Dixie Belle," reprinted from *Swing That Music*, by Louis Armstrong, published by Longmans Green and Company, Inc., used by permission of David McKay Company, Inc.

Harold Ober, Associates, Inc., for "Simple on Country Life," from *Book of Negro Folklore*, copyright © 1958 by Langston Hughes and Arna Bontemps.

Railroad Magazine, 205 East 42nd Street, New York, N.Y. 10017, for "Sim Webb's Account of the Wreck," in March 1936 issue of that magazine.

Russell & Volkening, Inc., Literary Agents, for "Louie Alexander," from *The Doctor to the Dead*, by John Bennett, copyright © 1946 by John Bennett.

Southern Folklore Quarterly for "The Witch Bridle," by John Harrington Cox, *Southern Folklore Quarterly*, Vol. 111, December 1943 (pp. 204–209).

The Texas Folklore Society for "The Devil in Texas," by Jovitá Gonzales in *Man, Bird and Beast*, pp. 102–109 (Publications of the Texas Folklore Society, VIII). For "Pipeline Days and Paul Bunyan," in *Follow de Drinkin' Gou'd*, pp. 55–61 (Publications of the Texas Folklore Society VIII).

University of Oklahoma Press for "Chief Cliff" and "The Origin of Fire," from *Indian Legends from the Northern Rockies*, by Ella E. Clark, copyright 1966 by the University of Oklahoma Press.

Vanguard Press, Inc., for selection from *The Hit*, by Julian Mayfield.

An extensive effort has been made to locate all persons having any rights or interests in the materials used in this collection and to clear reprint permissions with them. If any required acknowledgments have been omitted or any rights overlooked, it is contrary to our intention, and we would appreciate hearing from any copyright holder we have not been able to locate.

My special thanks to my wife Rosemary, whose devoted assistance is responsible for any virtues that may be found in this book.

Contents

III. TALES OF THE FRONTIER

IV. HEROES, REAL AND LEGENDARY

Paul Bunyan Stories

V. TALES OF THE SUPERNATURAL

VI. AMERICA SINGS

Introduction

Without becoming too technical, we may say that there are three general categories of literature in our country today. One is popular literature, which includes everything from comic books, magazines, and newspapers to radio, television and movies. Taken in this broad sense, popular literature can be read, heard or seen. This is the literature that you know best and feel most comfortable with. Its enormous influence is largely due to the mass media, which have spread "pop culture" to the most remote corners of our land.

Another is Literature with a capital L, the material which makes up the bulk of your high school English courses. It includes all the so-called "classic" novels, poems, short stories, plays, books of nonfiction and essays which are written and read by educated people. Whether you enjoy it or not, this type of literature is important because it usually reflects the accepted values and standards of our country. Since it does not depend on popular acceptance to survive, serious literature is relatively stable, and is therefore the means by which we transmit our cultural heritage from generation to generation.

The third, and probably least familiar to you, is oral or folk literature, the subject of this book. Strictly speaking, folklore is any material that exists in oral form and is passed on from person to person without benefit of being written down. As you well know, anything which is passed along by word of mouth is always being changed in its details, even though the essential part of it remains the same. A good example is the folk song "Barbara Allen," which has survived in oral tradition for hundreds of years. There are countless versions of "Barbara Allen," but almost all can be identified as the same song.

In the early stages of the development of a people, folklore is usually the only type of literature. With the invention of printing and other technological means of communication, it is superseded by popular and literary material. This was the case in our own country, before the coming of the white man. The American Indians were illiterate, and therefore depended entirely on oral material. The early settlers lacked leisure time, technology, and often literacy, and so they too relied heavily on oral tradition, much of it brought over from Great Britain and Europe. As the nation became settled, leisure time increased, public education taught nearly everyone to read and write, and twentieth-century technology made radio, television and recordings generally available. Today, oral literature in America has little significance. Fortunately, a dedicated army of folklorists has been scouring the backwaters of our country in recent years, collecting all the "pure" folk material before it is lost forever. Without them, much of the material in this book would have passed into an unwarranted oblivion.

Paradoxically, the decline of genuine folklore has been counterbalanced by a surge of interest on the part of Americans in their cultural heritage. Davy Crockett, Daniel Boone, and other historical figures whose exploits survived for years mainly in the oral tradition have been taken over by the mass media and "adapted" for children. Many nonhistorical folk characters, commonly thought of as folk heroes, probably never existed in oral tradition, but were created by professional writers to satisfy America's demand for a cultural heritage. Paul Bunyan, Pecos Bill, and Joe Magarac are examples of bogus folk heroes. Stories about these characters are rarely found among loggers, cowboys, or steelmen, where they supposedly originated. Richard M. Dorson coined the term "fakelore" to describe such material. While some of it may be quite worthwhile, it belongs definitely to the popular tradition.

Our literary tradition, too, has been heavily influenced by folklore. Melville made much use of whaling lore in *Moby Dick,* Mark Twain used his knowledge of Mississippi River lore in many of his books, and lesser writers like Bret Harte and James Fenimore Cooper drew on mining and Indian lore in much of their work.

While the literary and popular traditions have been making use of all the raw material provided for them by the oral tradition, true folklore has been largely neglected. Many of the selections in this book qualify as true folklore. They were written down only after many years of existence in the oral tradition, and are probably unfamiliar to most students. Others are not true folklore, but are literary works deriving from the oral tradition. A third group, such as the Bunyan stories, probably never existed in the oral tradition at all, but have become so generally accepted as folklore that their inclusion is justified. The student will probably be able to determine from the style in which each selection is written just how "authentic" it is. The real folklore may often be harder to read and may lack the polish of the more literary material, but may compensate for these defects with its honest, rough-hewn charm. Let the reader decide.

I

Toward the Present

The tremendous technological progress in our country over the past half-century has practically eliminated the need for an oral literature. Nearly everything worth preserving, and much that is not, is written down, recorded, or televised. Thus, many songs which once would have become part of an oral tradition enter the popular domain, performed by professional singers and protected from change by copyright laws. Today's legendary heroes do not spring up from the people, but are created by merchandisers who discover, through research into the mass mind, just what type of hero the American public craves. Witness the recent craze for superspies, which was really an attempt on the part of the mass media to capitalize on the enormous popularity of James Bond. Hordes of imitation James Bonds appeared, and the saturation point was soon reached. Yet no folklore about superspies appeared. It was all done *for* the people, whereas a true folk tradition depends on the *people* becoming actively involved in the creation and transmission of tales and songs.

This is not to say that Americans have abandoned hero worship. Certainly the late President Kennedy, the first astronauts, a few sports figures, and numerous entertainers are greatly admired by large segments of our population. Nevertheless, their lives have been so thoroughly documented by literature and the mass media that no significant body of oral material concerning these people has appeared. For this reason, most contemporary heroes, whatever their merits, really do not belong in a study of folklore. But men like Babe Ruth and Louis Armstrong, who became legendary in their own times, do merit inclusion in a folklore book.

It is evident that the student of American folklore must

direct most of his attention to the past. Nevertheless, there is still an oral tradition, and there always will be. Listen to any group of children jumping rope in the street, and you will hear any number of jingles, simple songs or sayings that accompany the activity. Most of what you hear has been passed on from generation to generation of children, through oral tradition.

What the reader will find in this part of the book, then, will not represent as great a wealth of folk literature as he will find in the later parts. What is included, however, should demonstrate that folklore in America still retains much of its old vitality.

THE LAVENDER EVENING DRESS
by Carl Carmer

"The Lavender Evening Dress" is one of the most widespread American folk tales. This version is a modern one, but the story has been with us for over a hundred years. A recent rock-and-roll version achieved great popularity.

A few years ago the postmaster in a village that lies beside the lonely waters of the Ramapo River, dappled by light and leaf shadow in the morning and darkened by hill shadows in the afternoon, talked often about a lithe tawny girl with hyacinth eyes and wheat-yellow hair. He was a sophisticated gentleman, traveled and urbane, a member of a distinguished family in those parts. To atone for his sins, he said, he taught a boys' class in a Sunday school that was in session on the first day of each week after the preaching in a tiny, weathered church back in the Ramapo hills.

From the summits of those hills, on a clear day washed by recent rain, the slim gray towers on Manhattan Island seem to advance into sight and hang, like figures long ago worked into the tapestry on the old blue sky wall. None of the boys in the Sunday school had ever entered the city on the horizon and only a few of them had been to Hillburn or Sloatsburg in New York State or any of the New Jersey towns to the west. They were a shy lot but wild as woods animals are wild, and they found the simple lessons in Christian ethics the postmaster was trying to teach difficult at best and impossible at those times when that girl was around.

She went through his class, the postmaster said, like a slow pestilence. A boy would be gone for a month, sometimes two months, and then he would come back on a Sunday, glowering and sheepish, and one of his schoolmates would be absent for a while. The Sunday-school teacher would sometimes see him and the girl picking wild blackberries on a hillside or, on a Saturday night, walking the road shoes in hand to a country dance.

There was much talk about the girl among the hill-folk gossips; and the postmaster, whose job gave him speaking acquaintance with most of these, gathered from what they said that she was gay and hot tempered and amoral—feeling that the general admiration gave her the privilege of disobeying the somewhat eccentric conventions of her own community. The only time he had a good look at her was during a Wednesday night prayer meeting at which, according to an announcement the previous Sunday, the contents of three barrels of old clothes from the members of a New York City church would be distributed. The girl came in after the service and just as the preacher beat in the head of the first barrel. She was barefoot and it was obvious that she wore only a stained and patched calico-check dress much too small for her. She sat in the back pew and paid no attention as the usual pathetic garments that are contained in such shipments were displayed and granted to those who could argue the greatest need.

There was a gasp when the preacher pulled from the middle of the second barrel a lavender evening dress covered with sequins that glinted like tiny amethysts. It was cut low off the shoulders and as soon as the preacher saw that he rolled it up into a shapeless bundle holding it helpless and waiting for someone to speak for it. No one did but the girl stood up and padded swiftly down the aisle. Without saying a word she grabbed the dress from the good man's hands and raced out of the church.

From that time on, the postmaster said, no one ever saw the girl in other costume. Rain or shine, day or night, she was a brush stroke of lavender against the brown of dirt roads, the green of hill slopes, the khaki-colored shirts and pants of whatever boy strode beside her.

Frost came early that year and leaves dropped. The air was clear and the New York towers came nearer and stayed longer. The hill people were all talking about a letter that had come to the girl from cousins in Jersey City. The postmaster had told one of his Sunday-school boys that the letter had come and the next day she had stood before his window and quietly asked for it, the sequins glinting purple in the shadowy room. People who dropped in the next day said her cousins had invited her to visit them and they had sent the money for her bus fare. A week later, a witness regaled the postmaster with a description of the expressions on the faces of the bus passengers down on the asphalt highway twelve miles away when the girl climbed aboard, holding her long skirt about her waist.

In mid-December came a cold snap and the thermometer outside showed eighteen degrees below zero when the postmaster opened his window for business. The people in the line of waiters-for-mail were more eager to give him the news than to receive their letters. The body of the girl in the lavender dress had been found frozen and stiff on the road a few miles above the bus stop. Returning from Jersey City, she had left the bus and begun the long walk home, but the evening dress proved too flimsy wear for such a night.

The postmaster said that after this tragedy all the students in his class came regularly to Sunday school, and that was the end of the story of the girl.

The girl froze to death about 1939 and for a decade nothing reflected doubt on the postmaster's conclusion. But now a growing number of people feel that his narrative, the truth of which is easily provable by many witnesses, has had an inexplicable consequence, overtones that have transcended his matter-of-fact realism. For a strange report recently began its rounds of upstate towns and, particularly, colleges. It had many variants, as such tales do, but in none of them was it in any way connected with the account of the girl, her dress, and her death, a factual record known only in the vicinity of her Ramapo home, and the suggestion of such a connection is made here possibly for the first time.

As I heard it, two Hamilton College juniors motoring to a dance at Tuxedo Park after sunset of a warm Indian summer Saturday on the road that runs through the valley of the little Ramapo River saw a girl waiting. She was wearing a party dress the color of the mist rising above the dark water of the stream and her hair was the color of ripe wheat. The boys stopped their car and asked the girl if they could take her in the direction she was going. She eagerly seated herself between them and asked if they were going to the square dance at Sterling Furnace. The thin, tanned face with high cheekbones, the yellow hair, the flashing smile, the quicksilver quality of her gestures, enchanted the boys and it was soon a matter of amused debate whether they would go along with her to Sterling Furnace or she would accompany them to the dance at Tuxedo. The majority won and the boys were soon presenting their new friend to the young couple who were their hosts at the Park. "Call me 'Lavender,' " she said to them. "It's my nickname because I always wear that color."

After an evening in which the girl, quiet and smiling, made a most favorable impression by her dancing, drifting dreamily through the waltzes in a sparkling cloud of lavender sequins, stepping more adeptly than any of the other dancers through the complications of revived square dances—Money Musk—Hull's Victory—Nellie Gray—the boys took her out to their car for the ride home. She said that she was cold and one of them doffed his tweed topcoat and helped her into it. They were both shocked into clichés of courtesy when, after gaily directing the driver through dusty woodland roads she finally bade him stop before a shack so dilapidated that it would have seemed deserted had it not been for a ragged lace curtain over the small window in the door. After promising to see them again soon, she waved good night, standing beside the road until they had turned around and rolled away. They were almost in Tuxedo before the chill air made the coatless one realize that he had forgotten to reclaim his property and they decided to return for it on their way back to college the next day.

The afternoon was clear and sunny when, after considerable difficulty in finding the shack, the boys knocked on the door with the ragged lace curtain over its window. A decrepit white-haired woman answered the door and peered at them out of piercing blue eyes when they asked for Lavender.

"Old friends of hers?" she asked, and the boys, fearing to get the girl into the bad graces of her family by telling the truth about their adventure of the day before, said yes they were old friends.

"Then ye couldn't a-heerd she's dead," said the woman. "Been in the graveyard down the road fer near ten years."

Horrified the boys protested that this was not the girl they meant—that they were trying to find someone they had seen the previous evening.

"Nobody else o' that name ever lived round here," said the woman. "Twan't her real name anyway. Her paw named her Lily when she was born. Some folks used to call her Lavender on account o' the pretty dress she wore all the time. She was buried in it."

The boys once more turned about and started for the paved highway. A hundred yards down the road the driver jammed on the brakes.

"There's the graveyard," he said, pointing to a few weathered stones standing in bright sunlight in an open field overgrown with weeds, "and just for the hell of it I'm going over there."

They found the stone—a little one marked "Lily"—and on the curving mound in front of it, neatly folded, the tweed topcoat.

New England Anecdotes

Many of the admired (but fast disappearing) character traits that came to be considered typically American originated with the New England Yankees. Shrewd, drily humorous, conservative, independent, hard-working, thrifty, unimpressed by pomp and greatness, and above all, stingy with words, the rural Yankee survives to this day as a genuine folk character. The following anecdotes illustrate some of his traits.

FANNY KEMBLE AND THE YANKEE FARMER

When Boston was Fanny Kemble's home, and her summers were spent here and there in rural Massachusetts, she engaged a worthy neighbor to be her charioteer during the season of one of her country sojournings. With kindhearted loquacity he was beginning to expatiate on the country, the crops and the history of the people roundabout, when Fanny remarked, in her imperious dogmatic fashion, "Sir, I have engaged you to drive for me, not to talk to me." The farmer ceased, pursed up his lips, and ever after kept his peace.

When the vacation weeks were over, and Miss Kemble was about to return to town, she sent for her Jehu and his bill. Running her eyes down its awkward columns, she paused. "What is this item, sir?" said she. "I cannot understand it." And with equal gravity he rejoined, "Sass, five dollars. I don't often take it, but when I do I charge."

THE RETURN OF THE NATIVE

by Kenneth L. Roberts

. . . A young man who had gone away from a New England village with his family at an early age returned after an absence of many years for the purpose of measuring the family woodlot. On his arrival he went to the post office to make certain inquiries of the postmaster, and on emerging from the post office he paused to pass the time of day with four or five old residents who were sitting on the post office steps, apparently allowing their minds to turn over silently in neutral, as one might say.

"Looks a little like rain," he remarked by way of an opening wedge.

His words were greeted with a rich silence on the part of the old residents.

"I say," he repeated, after something of a wait, "it looks as though it might rain."

After another long and eloquent silence, one of the natives removed his pipe from his mouth, neatly deluged an adjacent fly, turned his head slowly, gazed blankly at the young man, and finally asked:

"What you say yuh name wuz?"

"Why," said the young man, "my name's Eldridge. My family used to live over at Baxter's Dam Corners. Looks a little like rain, doesn't it?"

At this the silence again settled down over the post-office steps, but eventually the same inquisitive native once more turned his head and looked coldly at the stranger. "Any relation to Eben Eldridge?" he asked carelessly.

"Yes, indeed," said the young man. "Eben Eldridge was my uncle. We'll probably get a little rain, don't you think so?"

"Then your father wuz Herb Eldridge, wa'nt he?" asked the native.

"Yes, Herbert Eldridge was my father," the young man replied.

"Oh, that so!" said the native, deftly favoring another fly with a shower bath. "Eben Eldridge's nephew and Herb Eldridge's boy, hey? Hm! Well, well!"

He and his companions studied the toes of their shoes intently for a few moments, and finally the native looked up at the sky dubiously. "Well," he admitted with some reluctance, "it *may* rain."

INDEPENDENT VERMONTERS

by Keith W. Jennison

A Vermonter seldom hurries and he never wastes a motion. Vermont humor is like that—it ambles along, takes its time, and never wastes a word.

* * * * *

A theme of clannishness and rejection of the outsider runs through a lot of Vermont stories. One couple bought an old house and started down the road to find a man named Olin Warren who, they had been told, not only lived in the neighborhood but would be willing to make some basic repairs on the house. After walking about a half mile they saw a man cutting the roadside brush with a scythe.

"Do you know where Olin Warren lives?" asked the wife.

Without looking up the man said, "Yup."

They waited for further information. None came.

"Will you tell us where he lives?" the husband asked.

The man put down his scythe and pointed to a small house a mile up on the mountain.

"It's quite a walk," the husband continued. "You don't happen to know if he's home or not, do you?"

"Nope," said the man. "He ain't home." Then he looked at the couple for the first time. "What did you want with him?"

"Well," said the wife, "we bought the old Gokey place down the road and somebody told us Olin Warren might be willing to do some repairing for us."

The man rested his scythe for a moment. "I be he," he said.

*　　*　　*　　*　　*

As is true in most states, there are really two Vermonts. One is the new Vermont that has grown up along the tourist routes and makes its living supplying consumer goods to travelers. I include ski slopes in this category. The other is the old rural Vermont that hasn't changed much for more than two hundred years. The line dividing the two is indistinct, however, for it is still possible to ask for an advertised item in a store and be told it is not kept in stock because it sells too fast.

The matter of scenery comes in for a good deal of comment for, of course, it looks different to the tourist than it does to the native. One visitor exclaimed over the beauty of a certain vista, only to get the following response:

"Well, maybe, but if you had to fence that view, plow it, plant it, hoe it, mow it, and pay taxes on it—it would look pretty durned ugly."

The ornery quality of Vermont humor is not always directed toward strangers. One man came back to his home town after what he considered an illustrious career in New York. To his surprise, there was nobody at the station to meet him. Finally he found the station master asleep on a baggage truck on the shady side of the station. Upon being awakened, the station master looked up, rubbed his eyes, and said:

"Why, hello, Johnny, going some place?"

Another Vermonter took a trip of a completely different nature. He lived in Vermont close to the New Hampshire border. The survey for a new road, however, disclosed that his farm actually had always been on the New Hampshire side of the line. When he was told this, he said.

"Well, thank the good God almighty, I couldn't have stood another of them Vermont winters."

Some of the old trades aren't practiced anymore. Blacksmiths, for example, are hard to find. But one out-of-state motorist managed to find one within a mile of the place where his car had broken down. He explained his trouble and asked the blacksmith if he thought he could fix it.

"Sure," said the blacksmith. "I do everything from shoeing horses—on down."

With Vermont's new look as one of America's favorite summer and winter playgrounds, you don't hear as much of the biting humor as you used to. It never really dies out, though. . . .

Although you couldn't get one to admit it, the answer most Vermonters feel is the truest was made in response to a question asked by a visitor. Looking out over a hillside where the flint and slate edges cut up through the thin soil, this stranger had said:

"Doesn't look like much of a farming country around here. What do you raise?"

The farmer looked at him steadily. "Men," he said.

Tales and Poems of Negro Life

Cut off from the mainstream of American culture, the ghetto Negro has developed a folklore of his own. These tales and poems show how far from the American dream he is. Yet the richness of the language compares favorably with that of the best American folklore.

THE HIT

by Julian Mayfield

The most popular gambling game in New York City, and especially in Harlem, is the numbers. The poorest, most miserable creature alive can play. To try his luck, all he needs is a penny, and if his guess is right the numbers bank will pay him six dollars in return. The odds against his winning are a thousand to one, and his payoff is only six hundred to one, but this disparity is somewhat compensated for by the comparative ease with which he can play this supposedly illegal game. The fat lady upstairs who sits at home all day with her cats and dogs, the grasping little man in the candy store across the street, the furtive, overdressed loafer with glistening shoes who is standing on the corner at sunrise—each will take a bet on the numbers. The penny bet is the stock in trade of a multi-million-dollar business with its headquarters downtown in the city's financial district. This business is incorporated, after a fashion; it has its stockholders, its officers, its workers, and its payroll. Its volume of business is steady, and it is seldom in crisis, for it is based on that most solid and persistent of all American phenomena—the dream.

Noon eased itself into the Manhattan streets. The sun hung high over Harlem, and its heat was heavy as a white cloak over the flat roofs and the gray streets. Children sought the coolness of dark basements and dark hallways. The old people sat near their windows and looked with indifference out onto the shimmering streets. Behind the lunch counters brown girls and yellow girls, irritated by the heat and their own perspiration, grouchily served up frankfurters with sauerkraut, hot sausages with mustard and relish and onion, milk shakes, malteds, coffee, and orange juice; served these to impatient clerks and laborers and helpers' helpers, to shoppers, policemen, and hack drivers. Preachers napped and dreamed of churches larger than the Abyssinian. Lawyers and petty real-estate brokers planned and schemed and gamblers figured. A con man dropped a wallet with a hundred-dollar bill in it to the sidewalk in front of the Corn Exchange Bank and waited for a sucker to fall for the age-old game. A hustler sat in her apartment on Sugar Hill sipping cocktails with a white merchant from downtown who was taking a long week end, sized him up, estimated his worth. Madam Lawson shuffled her cards, Madam Fatima stared into her silver crystal ball, and turbaned Abdul Ben Said of the ebony skin mumbled an incantation to the black gods of old, and lo! all of them saw glory in the morning if not sooner. There, near the top of Manhattan Island, Harlem sizzled and baked and groaned and rekindled its dream under the midday sun.

And so the great dream machine was wound tight. The nickels were in the slots and the players waited. Only a turn of the handle was needed to set the whole thing in motion.

Oh, Lord, please let that number be 316 today. You know my life ain't been easy, me with three mouths to feed and that man of mine done snuck away like a dirty little coward. I done forgive him, Lord, the way I know You wanted me to—I never think no evil of him no more. But it's hard trying to feed these three kids on thirty dollars a week. Now, with a twenty-five cent hit I could get shoes for little Johnny and Mary and Sarah Lou, and clothes to keep them in school . . . So if you please, Lord, let that number come 316. . . .

A girl needs nice things or men just look the other way . . . dresses, slips, a handbag . . . Honest to goodness, I'm out of just about everything. Just can't seem to make enough to keep up. But if I can hit 212 today . . .

How a man can work so hard and never have any money I just don't know. If that 530 don't come today, I just don't know what I'm going to do. There's the television set to be paid, the refrigerator, the furniture and the car, all of which comes due the first of the month. Not to mention the rent that never stops and the gas and electricity and the telephone. I could take care of these things if 530 was to jump out just the way I played it.

Let 728 come, and Harlem's gonna wake up and find out that I am here. I'll rent myself a suite up on the top floor of the Theresa and throw a party that will last a week. Then I'll buy myself the prettiest Cadillac Harlem ever saw. It'll even have a television set in it. I might even send some money to Mama down home, too. She ain't been doing so good lately. . . .

Lord, I'm needing a new church so as I can help set these people back on the path of righteousness. I saw a nice big store at One hundred and thirty-sixth and Lenox, and I have made inquiries, and I know that store can be acquired for a hundred and twenty-five a month. Now, they want two months in advance, and You know I don't have that kind of money. It's the perfect site for the Blessed Lamb Holiness Church.

From there, Lord, the truth of Your loving word will flow all over Harlem and bring these wayward sheep back to the fold. The number is 471, Lord, and I have played it in a six-way combination. Now, if in Your loving kindness You could see fit to make things go that way, O Lord, we would be eternally in Your debt as we are already. All these things we ask in Jesus' name.

Amen.

SISTER LUCY
(*Fragment of a funeral sermon*)

I seen our sister in life,
An' she done her duty,
She served her God
An' done her earthly labor
As best she knowed how,
An' listened for the blowin' of the trumpet.
Death had no fears for her,
For the blowin' of the trumpet,
The Master's trumpet,
Was the music that she loved;
The blowin', the blowin' of the trumpet,
The Master's trumpet.

At the mornin' sunrise,
She was on her row,
An' when the sun had set,
Her daily task was done;
An' when the night was come
She knelt in prayer beside her bed
An' listened for the blowin' of the trumpet,
The Master's trumpet.

The music that she loved,
The blowin', the blowin' of the trumpet,
The Master's trumpet.

She had met the world
Wid strength an' grace;
Although her life was trailed by hardship,
Love was in her heart for man
An' in her soul for God.
An' she listened for the blowin' of the trumpet.
The Master's trumpet,
The music that she loved,
The blowin', the blowin' of the trumpet,
The Master's trumpet.

Wid a frosty life behind her,
Wid misery savage
As a hungry hound
Ever wid her,
She never lost her faith in God,
An' she listened for the blowin' of the trumpet.
The Master's trumpet,
The music that she loved,
The blowin', the blowin' of the trumpet,
The Master's trumpet.

THE BAREFOOT PROPHET
by *Abram Hill*

In the years gone by . . . prophets have appeared in Harlem representing the whole list of Biblical oracles, all of them with "calls" and supernatural credentials. Martin was the first to be known simply as "The Prophet." He was probably Harlem's most picturesque figure. Watching him stroll along the avenue was a pleasant thing to behold. His luxuriant mane of gray hair and flowing beard made him look as if he had just stepped from the pages of the Bible.

Prophet Martin was a beloved man and a one-man institution. He carried the word daily to stranger places than street corners. Patrons were seldom surprised to see him in gin mills, cabarets, bars or buffet flats. Usually he would quote a few passages of the Scriptures, take up a small collection, and then vanish. Small children followed him through the streets, touching his robe for "good luck." Confused parents would stop him in the streets and seek advice about their wayward offspring. Hustlers and number runners treated him with respect and unsmilingly accepted his benedictions.

Legends grew. It was rumored that he was rich; that he owned several apartment houses and that he traveled over the country in an expensive automobile. This Prophet Martin denied emphatically. He pointed out that he never accepted a church. He had no income other than the small change that he received from his listeners. He preached on the street corners for fifty years in twenty-five different states. When he died his family was on relief.

"The Prophet" was born Clayburn Martin in Henry County, Virginia, in 1851. At an early age he had a vision. "Take off your shoes, for this is holy ground. Go preach My gospel," a voice told him. He obeyed. His first audience was a group of crap shooters on a street corner. He succeeded in influencing the crap shooters so well that he continued his mission.

Mary, his wife, was over twenty years his junior. He had four daughters and one son. The latter was born when he was sixty-one years of age. Once he grew weak and listened to Mary. She told him to cut his hair and wear shoes. Like Samson he cut his locks. Illness followed. He realized his error. He let his hair grow back and again trod his way in bare feet.

His health was restored and he never cut his locks nor wore shoes again.

The vagabond preacher maintained a sanctum sanctorum at 217 West 134th Street. He received callers every evening from 6 to 8:30. Brother Russell, himself a living witness to the healing power of Prophet Martin, would assist him. Here "The Prophet" would ask whether the trouble was of the soul or of the body. If it was of the soul, confession and prayer were enough. If God's Temple—that is what he called the body—was broken down, he would administer a few drops of the ointment or drugs which he prepared himself, then console the ailing person with a few words of prayer. Once he was arrested in Newark, New Jersey, for practicing medicine without a license.

"I will make you ruler over the Nations. I will lift up my people through you," he would begin. Though he could not read nor write, God gave him his messages. "You are the temples. Every man is the dwelling place of the Almighty. He's not in the buildings we call churches." Thus he justified his nonbelief in church buildings.

The title of Elder was bestowed by "The Church of God, Pillar, Ground of Truth, House for all people, Holy and Sanctified."

Prophet Martin's short messages showed a great lyrical quality, somewhat in the style of James Weldon Johnson's "Creation." Following is one of Martin's typical sermons:

Our world is like a fox, brethren. Like a fox that catch his foot in the trap of the Devil. Fox knows, brethrens, that if he stays long enough in the Devil's trap the Devil will kill him with a long stick. So the fox gnaws off his foot and leaves the foot for the Devil and goes home on three legs and praises God he's gettin home at all.

Now brethren, you see what I mean. We got sin and we got sinners, and better than that the sinners should lead us into the Devil's trap we must cut them off. Sin ain't no part of God, my brethren, but we righteous are part of God Himself. We got to save all we can, and let the rest go. But now, brethren, before we let 'em go, let's pray hard and long for them with His omnipresence.

Prophet Martin died in July, 1937. He was eighty-six years old. Barefooted in death as he was in life, his bushy head resting on a royal purple cushion, the aged evangelist lay in state. Hundreds heeded a last message pinned to the box, resting on his chest. The appeal written in his own shaking hand as he lay dying in Harlem Hospital read:

"Help bury the prophet."

PAWNSHOP BLUES

by Brownie McGhee

Well, I'm walkin' down the street this mornin',
Hear someone call my name and I could not stop,
Someone called me and I could not stop,
Well, boys, you know Brownie was broke and hungry,
On my way to that old pawnshop.

Well, I went to the pawnshop, had my last suit in my hand,
Yes, I went to the pawnshop,
Had my last suit of clothes in my hand,
I said, "won't you give me a loan?
Try to help me, Mister Pawnshop Man."

Well, I went to the pawnshop,
Went down to pawn my radio,
Went down to pawn my radio,
Well, the man said, "Brownie, you ain't got a T.V.—
We don't take radios in no more."

Well, I went to the pawnshop,
'Cause the man had come and took my car.
You know I had lost my job, man, that car man took my car.
Well, I'm goin' to the pawnshop in the mornin'
See if I can pawn my old guitar.

I asked the pawnshop man
What was those three balls doin' on the wall,
What was those three balls doin' on the wall.
"Well, I bet you two to one, buddy,
You won't get your stuff out o' here at all."

SIMPLE ON COUNTRY LIFE
by Langston Hughes

"A man might only live to be seventy or eighty years old," said Simple, "and that is too short a time to waste in the country."

"What do you mean, waste it in the country?" I asked.

"I mean eighty years is too short a time to even be going to the country on vacations," said Simple. " I do not see any use wasting my life in the rurals when I can stay in New York City, Harlem, and have four times as much fun. In the country there is nothing to see but nature. In the city you can look at peoples. In the country there may be chickens, but in town there are chicks. In the country, there is moonlight, but I'll take neon signs for mine. Besides the country is dangerous."

"Dangerous?"

"A man might get snake-bit," said Simple, "else stung in the eye by a bee, or on the elbow by a wasp, maybe even on the bohunkus by a hornet. Oh, no, I do not like country! There are too many varmints there."

"In the American countryside," I said, "there are very few harmful animals."

"No, but there are mosquitoes," said Simple, "and they are vicious enough. I was setting on a porch swing with a girl out in the country down in Virginia one night when a mosquito stung me so hard I thought that chick had stuck a hatpin in my arm. Mosquitoes go for blood. They can also make a man a nervous wretch. Z-zzz-zz-z—they sound like dive bombers. Mosquitoes can make romance in the dark a nightmare. Then in the daytime in the country there are all kinds of flies, but worse of all is horseflies. Daddy-o, if you have never been stung by a horsefly, you have not been stung at all! To tell the truth, a horsefly does not even sting, it bites. And there are little old pesky sandflies and buzzflies and bottleflies and waterflies. Man, I see no need to go to the country where all them flies is when I can stay right here on Lenox Avenue and be bothered with nothing but butterflies—whose bark is worse than their bite.

"And speaking of barks, fellow, every farmer in the country has two or three big, bad, loud-barking dogs, some of which will rush at a stranger out taking a quiet walk and try to tear his leg off. There is nothing more fiercer than a country dog, be it fice or hound. And don't let the dog be one of them bristly haired mongrel kind whose fur stands up like a porcupine when he sees a Negro like me coming down the road. Sometimes I think country dogs are race prejudiced. I seed a dog down in Tidewater once, the darker a Negro was, the louder he would bark at him. Of course, that dog belonged to a very mean old white man, so I reckon it were trained to express prejudice. Well, anyhow, one reason I do not like the country is on account of loose dogs. In Harlem dogs have to be on a leash, else have a muzzle if they run loose in the parks and I have heard of nobody yet being bit by a dog in front of the Hotel Theresa. But in front of almost any farmhouse, a man just minding his own business is likely to be dogbit. I do not wish to run that risk by spending my vacation in the country. Fresh air or no fresh air, I do not want to get hydrophobia."

"You exaggerate the dangers of the country," I said. "Thousands of city folks go to the hinterlands for vacations."

"Hinter I will not go," said Simple. "Let whomsoever will go hinter, but not I. Another thing, there is no sidewalks in the country. Rain comes, you wade in the mud. There are no street lights. Dark comes, you fumble home the best way you can. There are no licker stores. Drink up what drinks you brought with you—and from there on in you get along the best way you can—just go dry, or drink spring water, of which I had enough in my youthhood. Also, it can get *so* lonesome at night in the country. And who says it is quiet? Crickets chirping, frogs croaking, mosquitoes buzzing, cows bawling, dogs howling, chickens crowing long before day. Oh, no, man, no! I can sleep much better in town with nothing but taxis going by, fire engines screeching, neighbors cursing, and folks fighting outside my windows. Them is *natural* noises. But country noises of things in the dark unseen, them kind of noises can make the hair rise on your head. I do not like no noise I cannot spy with my eye if I want to, guy—which is why, let all who wish go to the country. NOT I! Period! NOT I!"

BABE RUTH
by Paul Gallico

If any sports figure can be called legendary, George Herman "Babe" Ruth (1895-1948) is the best candidate. An orphan, Ruth rose to the top in the best American tradition of skill, bravado, and determination. Although baseball records are surpassed every year, public indignation erupted several years ago when Roger Maris hit 61 home runs in one season, one more than the number Ruth hit in 1927. Finally, an asterisk was entered next to Maris' record, noting that Babe Ruth had set his record in 154 games, whereas it took Maris 162 games to break it. Since no other record has received this considera- tion, the veneration in which Ruth is still held is obvious.

When first I blocked out this series and sat down to plan the inclusion of those I remembered with the greatest warmth and pleasure, men and women who had provided me with not only copy, but thrills and enjoyment over the years distilled from their personalities as well as from their prowess, the first name I put down was that of George Her- man (Babe) Ruth.

He was Number One. No weighing-up, no shillyshally- ing comparisons. There he stood before me in belted camel's hair coat and cap, a friendly, sardonic grin spreading all over his ugly map and his rumbling laugh bubbling up from his vast interior. Although he had been dead for sixteen years, he was as alive and vital to me as in the days when I was trav- eling on the Yankee Special. I played handball with him in Jack O'Brien's gymnasium during the winter months. In the summer, from my eyrie in the press box, I watched and mar- veled as he boomed the ball over the walls of the stadia of New York, Washington, Boston, Detroit, and other arenas of the American League circuit, to be retrieved by some urchin far out on Railroad Avenue and kept by him forever as an object of veneration. Once more I felt the curious thrill of affection this man engendered in all of us who were associ- ated with him and who were his Boswells.

Looking backward, I see the figure of Ruth during his years with the Yankees far from being paled by the passage of time. On the contrary, for me the light he once shed if any- thing burns still more brightly. He was Gargantua in human form. No one has appeared upon the scene since his death to match him or give us any cause either to diminish or forget him.

During the baseball season from April to the World Series at the beginning of October, and often a good part of the winter months as well, the Babe lived with us daily and we with him until he became a better-known and better-publicized figure even than the President of the United States. He could not have achieved this had he not been worthy of it, had he not been the extraordinary figure he was with the capacity to make men, small boys, and even women love and care about him.

It has been said that people like Ruth, Dempsey, Tunney, Tilden, and all the sensational champions of the era, were made by newspaper ballyhoo, the opening up of newspaper columns and the increasing number of sports pages. But this is not so. Looking back upon the turmoil and the hubbub from the vantage of retrospect there is no doubt in my mind which came first, the chicken or the egg.

It was the characters that made people care deeply. The newspapers discovered that caring meant circulation, which brought advertising and advertising a share of the rich, ripe melon we were cutting up in our postwar spree.

In times past we had been interested in and excited by prize fighters and baseball players, but we had never been so individually involved or joined in such a mass outpouring of affection as we did for Ruth.

It seemed as though after the war we looked upon almost everything and everyone in sports with quite different eyes than we did at the century's turn. There was, of course, the usual postwar population explosion, but more than this, we felt we had earned the right to substitute the gaiety and thrill of sports combat for the real thing that we wanted to forget.

Editors were supposed to be sensitive to the public pulse. They were indeed. They opened up the pages to this different kind of hero or heroine, and into this newly created vacuum strode the giants. The newspapers that followed their careers most closely were rewarded with soaring sales and circulation figures. The big, black headline, as strident as those reporting any form of battle action, "BABE HITS NOS. 32 & 33," rolled from the presses and came out as gold and silver.

If the Babe had not been the Babe, the man, the character, the personality he was, he might have passed merely as an exceptional hitter.

It was the caring about him that counted.

During that resplendent decade and a little beyond, Babe Ruth compiled his fabulous record of 714 home runs in his lifetime; 60 in one season; 11 seasons of more than 40 home runs, as well as a lifetime collection of 2056 bases on balls and 1330 strikeouts, and at the same time became a living legend and the best-known, most loved baseball player of all time.

This is to take nothing from your Roger Maris, who hit 61 home runs in 162 games, a remarkable feat indicative of a fine athlete and a splendid batter.

Yet there is one great difference between the extravagant sets of home runs hit by Babe Ruth and Roger Maris. For the latter was a pursuit, an attempt to surpass which produced some stirring tensions, but the way led through known territory. Someone had been there before and established the fact that it was possible. The home runs amassed by Babe Ruth, and in particular his great record of 60 in 154 games, was the sheerest pioneering and exploration into the uncharted wildernesses of sport. There was something almost of the supernatural and the miraculous connected with him, too. And this in turn had much to do with us, the ebullience of our times, the exuberance and the joy of living. Our music, literature, and drama reflected this lighthearted pleasure and so did the ceaseless click of the hits off the bat of the Babe, a kind of metronome to our success.

The Babe was a bundle of paradoxes. Somehow one of the most appealing things about him was that he was neither built, nor did he look like an athlete. He did not even look like a ballplayer. Although he stood six feet two inches and weighed 220 pounds, his body was pear-shaped and even when in tip-top condition he had a bit of a belly. His barrel always seemed too much for his legs, which tapered into a pair of ankles as slender almost as those of a girl. The great head perched upon a pair of round and unathletic shoulders, presented a moon of a face, the feature of which was the flaring nostrils of a nose that was rather like a snout. His voice was deep and hoarse, his speech crude and earthy, his ever-ready laughter a great, rumbling gurgle that arose from the caverns of his middle. He had an eye that was abnormally quick, nerves and muscular reactions to match, a supple wrist, a murderous swing, and a gorgeously truculent, competitive spirit.

Maris, for instance, must be similarly endowed strength-and reactionwise, but they say that Roger is a cold fish and nothing rides his long ball but power. There was always an emotion of some kind accompanying the Babe's home run hit as it departed from the premises. No ballplayer to my knowledge or recollection, with the possible exception of Willie Mays, ever delivered the goods with such infectious gusto, or more greatly enjoyed his abilities and his sucesses. Life for the Babe consisted of women, food, liquor, and baseball, and when his appetites for the first three were appeased, there was nothing that gave him more intense satisfaction than whipping the ball out of the playing field, and no one ever put more effort into the attempt.

This love of and delight in accomplishment spread to the spectators in the stands. His rooters savored his triumphs vicariously; his enemies reveled in his failures. For his misses were as prodigious as his hits. At the end of a swung strike his legs would be braided like a barroom pretzel, and he would be facing three-quarters of the compass around from where he had started.

It was the unique capacity of the Babe's warm, extravagant, vital personality which enabled the onlookers to play the game with him, to share his feelings, his fervor, and above all his implacable intent as, standing over the plate, he peered out toward the mound and menaced the pitcher with a preliminary wave or two of his bat. At that moment in a packed Yankee Stadium we all became one with him, 70,000 Ruths of us on the big days, equipped with the determination and extraordinary power to wreck the ball game. There took place a transference in which the least and humblest nobody in the stands found himself swelling with the magnificent afflatus of the Babe.

It was our decade that Ruth was expressing, the golden touch, the can't-be-beaten, the we-can-do-it, the key to success and wealth, money in the pocket and two chickens in every pot.

When the famous, dry "click" was heard as the white ball arched and fielders stood with their hands helplessly placed upon their hips, their heads turned for a last farewell glimpse of the departing sphere, the great roar that exploded from the stands was for the Babe, but the salute was also to the unconquerable, unquenchable us. We had done it again.

You might think, perhaps, that this plethora of home runs would cheapen them and satiate our appetites. Far from it; every time Ruth came to bat he was on his way to some kind of record. Every ball he expelled from the stadia was one more link in the chain of continuing and progressing miracles. The impossible was becoming the probable, and for the price of admission would take place before one's very eyes. And the Babe's utter demolishing of every prior home run record was just another verification of the opulence of our times.

The home run, then, during the rule of Ruth became in

a way the equivalent of the jackpot. It disgorged runs in showers and the arch-Croesus of this largess was the weird-looking man with the barrel body, spindly legs, and pudding face. For though the denigrators will talk about the advent of the rabbit ball and the explosive center, the fact remains that during the early days of the decade when Ruth was already racking up forty or more home runs, nobody else was hitting them—certainly not that many, until the coming of Lou Gehrig. Home runs flowed from his bat the way gold was supposed to pour from the cornucopia of the Goddess of Plenty.

Baseball, of course, is a team game: nine men acting in concert to expunge the batter; batters collaborating their efforts in sucession to throw the defense out of gear, put runners on base, advance them, and turn them into runs. But Ruth additionally always had a private duel with the pitcher. In fact most of the great man's effort was concentrated upon an unaided performance. If he connected, he needed no further assistance to get him around the bases. Any player who had the good fortune to be on ahead of him, came home automatically as the Babe dogtrotted around the bases, doffing his cap. With rare exceptions his home runs were such complete affairs that there was no call for speed, or even the semblance of running.

The game, as you know, is so constituted that a runner who lags on the bases may be tagged out by a member of the opposing team, if he has the ball in his hands. But after Ruth had applied his magic bat to a missile, there simply was no more ball with which to tag anyone. It was either in the pocket of some delirious fan in the right-field bleachers, or rolling along in the gutter of a thoroughfare outside the ball park. A new one had to be produced before the game could continue. Ruth conceded touching the bases as he jogged around them, in the manner of royalty acknowledging ancient protocol or formality.

This left the combat area largely up to Ruth at the plate with the opposing pitcher on the mound. And never before had the spectators at ball games and all those who attended them vicariously through their newspapers or their just-budding radio sets, become quite so aware of the nature of the struggle between the thrower and the hitter.

The man on the mound had a bag of tricks at his disposal. He could throw the ball with blinding speed, or float it deceptively. He could make it swoop, yaw, drop, sail, or, soaped with saliva, break maniacally before the plate in a manner that no man could foresee.

Against this highly scientific hocus-pocus of imparting spin and unorthodox behavior to a ball in flight, the batter had to respond with a camera-lens eye and photo-flash reaction.

Now none of this is news to the baseball fan, nor is it intended to be. It is only to remind him of the extent to which the situation of George Herman Ruth at bat and any one of a hundred pitchers on the mound, became such a personal affair. The Babe was not interested in being presented with four balls and a walk. He was not looking to bloop a single into short center, or even drive a double between two outfielders. His sole ambition was to lace that ball out of the park and, singlehandedly, contribute from one to four runs at a time. The pitcher's aim and desire was to prevent this, to force him into three prodigious whiffies, or to slide the third one across between shoulder and knees with the big bat still on the Babe's shoulders. Let it be said here and now that the pitcher's problem was further complicated by the fact that prior to this time, none of them had ever encountered so dangerous and miraculous a hitter. It undoubtedly worked upon their nerves. It was unfair to bring magic into baseball. In a way it was something like fighting against the man who wielded the sword named "Excalibur." It gave him an edge.

And this was something new in sports, wholly and utterly novel, never before seen on any baseball diamond; something akin to the unstoppable force meeting the immovable object. For the first time in the not-too-long history of the game, the pitcher was throwing to a man who was capable of breaking up the ball game at any moment. Day in and day out we watched these duels with unflagging excitement and exaltation and all of America watched too. At the hour of Evensong the question would arise upon millions and millions of lips, "Did the Babe hit one today?"

Ruth had a fine, ruffianly sense of humor. He was able to laugh at himself, particularly after a prodigious strikeout. But there was no laughter that became him better than the rumbling gurgle of satisfaction following upon that brief explosion, signaling the fact that the opposition had guessed wrong and he had guessed right.

The Ruthian humor was not restricted only to the demolishment of the pride of the man on the mound, it went further than that. It must be remembered that the pitcher, while it is his strength and skill that speeds the ball, collaborates with the catcher, who calls by secret sign for the kind of delivery he thinks will do the trick. This catcher, also by signal, is frequently in communication with the Great Brain, the manager on the bench.

The Babe happily thought, and often spoke, aided by the four-letter word. When he connected and the ball hissed its farewell in the sky as he trotted around the base paths, the Babe was supremely and ecstatically content in the fact that he had given a four-letter wording to all three, pitcher, catcher, manager. This joy was so visibly effulgent and effervescent, the four-letter word was so evidently hovering about his head or shimmering over the field as he toured the bases, even though his lips might not be moving, that it was communicated to us in an exquisite and relaxing catharsis. Some part of this wonderful feeling spread to every corner of the United States.

There was something else that helped to make for the enormous, vicarious enjoyment the masses derived out of Babe Ruth's performances on and off the diamond. For not only did he not look like an athlete, neither did he behave like one. There had been big leaguers before and will have been since, who suffered from too great an attraction to the bottle, the flesh, or the dinner table, but never one who so heartily indulged in and relished all three as Babe Ruth.

Thus he became the beloved alter ego of every man who wished himself able to stuff, drink, wench, and still come through. Ruth could and did. He broke every training rule and regulation that ever was included in *mens sana in corpore sano* and still pulled those booming, luscious, satisfying home runs off his bat, made impossible catches in the field, and threw strikes into the catcher's mitt to cut off runs at the plate with his bottom backed into the right-field wall.

A glimpse into baseball records will fill you in on the staggering "firsts" and "mosts" of the lifetime averages of the Babe in a career that stretched from 1914 to 1935. One could dizzy you with figures, but looking backward I find now, as then, that I am still far more interested in what this man meant to us and the strange love we all felt for him.

For this affection was not confined only to baseball fans or spectators. He was loved by millions of Americans who had never seen him play or, for that matter, even attended a ball game. Somehow Ruth had come to be regarded as a member of everyone's family, and we were concerned with his troubles and his problems as well as his successes, as though he was one of our own children. Like a child he was frequently naughty. The whole of the United States shared in his public punishments. When he was ill we all suffered with and for him and watched by his hospital bedside. When he was fined and suspended for insubordination and breaking training, we shuddered and sympathized. And there was that fantastic day in Chicago, when Root of the Cubs had two strikes on him and the Babe called his shot by pointing to the flagpole in center field and then hit the next pitch to the very same spot for a home run. Not only the World Series crowd and those of us in the press box, but practically every home in America thrilled as though the feat had been accomplished by our own son.

The Babe lived—well and heartily. He seemed to be filled with a mischievous joy and appreciation of all of the good things in life, and surely it was this great zest and enthusiasm which enabled Ruth to give so prodigiously when playing his game. His impish streak was at the bottom of the delight he took in the discomfiture of every pitcher who had thrown him a home run ball.

No doubt his antecedents and his rise, again an example of the great American success story, helped to inspire the outpourings of love from the masses of his admirers. For a poor and intractable boy who had spent the greater part of his youth in a reform school for incorrigibles, he had come a long way and had earned the particular doting worship of gamins who, invariably, wherever he appeared, furnished the tail to his meteor-like presence. He had a feeling for children and consented genially to be their god. He was the hero of the millions like himself who were poor, neglected, and unsung, the messiah of the underprivileged and wretched young, and every time he went to bat he delivered an unmistakable sermon, "Ye, too, may enter into the Kingdom of Swat."

A baseball autographed by him became a unique and venerable object to be enshrined in the home. For a small boy to meet or touch him was to be suffused with the radiance and the glory, and the Babe even became endowed with powers of healing. If anyone should be looking to canonize a saint of baseball there are authentic records, all during our times, of Ruth saving the life of this or that sick child by a hospital bedside visit and the promise to hit a home run especially for him, and one which he always managed to keep.[1]

The sympathetic magic of the Babe extended even to the spectator in the stands. For after seeing a Ruthian homer one came away with a kind of ineffable glow in one's middle, and for a long time afterward had the feeling of something wonderful having happened that day.

Has there been a ballplayer since his era who has had such a grip upon the affection of the nation? I would think no. Not only has no such extraordinary figure appeared upon the sports scene, but our times and we, too, as people, have changed. Casting backward to the innocence of the decade between 1920 and 1930, we know now that our world of today has turned savage, cruel, and inhospitable. We are menaced from within and without and beset with fears, worries, and situations we have never had to face before. We have lost some of that capacity to care deeply about anyone or anything besides our immediate families. The fact that once there was an easier age, that there was such a man as Ruth when we were young and that he so endeared himself to us was really what was good about those old days.

[1]As a matter of fact, many years later I did canonize him in a short story called "Saint Bambino." I wrote this one sentimental evening some ten years after his death. As I remember it I had been listening to a World Series broadcast over the Armed Forces Network which reached me where I was living, isolated on a mountaintop in Liechtenstein. Suddenly I was aware of a great nostalgia for those times and for the Babe himself, and set to work. Sometimes fiction succeeds even better than fact in re-creating a character and bringing him to life. . . .

LOUIS ARMSTRONG ON THE *DIXIE BELLE*

Louis Armstrong, born in 1900, is probably the best known jazz personality in the world today. A leading exponent of the Dixieland style, he has truly become a legend in his own lifetime. "Louis Armstrong on the Dixie Belle*" relates how he got his start as a jazzman. "Louis Armstrong on Oliver" is a last tribute to Joe Oliver, his friend and mentor.*

My river life on [the *Dixie Belle*] (it lasted for two years) is one of my happiest memories and was very valuable to me. It all grew out of a funny accident—another of the breaks I said I have had. Kid Ory's Band had been engaged one evening to play on a truck that was to drive through the streets advertising some big dance. They were always advertising like that with trucks and bands in New Orleans. Well, we were playing a red-hot tune when another truck came along the street with another hot band. We came together at that same corner of Rampart and Perdido Streets where I had been arrested five years before and sent to the Waif's Home. Of course that meant war between the two bands and we went to it, playing our strongest. I remember I almost blew my brains through my trumpet.

A man was standing on the corner listening to the "fight." When we had finally outplayed the other band, this man walked over and said he wanted to speak with me. It was "Fate" Marable, a noted hot pianist and leader of the big band on the excursion steamer *Dixie Belle*. He said he had heard me blow and wanted me for his band. It was in November of 1919. I had been with Kid Ory at the Peter Lalas Cabaret at Iberville and Maris Streets for sixteen months. I had learned a lot from Ory and had begun to get a little reputation, in a small sort of way, as a hot trumpeter. But while I could play music, like most of the others I couldn't read it much yet—just a little. I had made my mind up I wanted to learn.

It may sound funny that I was so quick to leave Kid Ory and sign up for the boat with "Fate" Marable, as though I were just running out on Ory after the big chance he had put my way and all he had done for me. The excursion boats had a big name in those days. They played the Mississippi ports away up to St. Paul and beyond. When they went North on these trips they always had white orchestras but for the first time it was planned that year to take a colored orchestra along on the *Dixie Belle* when she shoved off in the spring on her trip North. I guess that was because the colored orchestras that had been coming up strong in New Orleans in the last few years, like Kid Ory's, were so hot and good that they were getting a real reputation. The chance to be with that first colored jazz band to go North on the river might have turned any kid's head at nineteen. But even that wouldn't have been enough to make me leave Ory. I wanted to get away from New Orleans for another reason and that was because I was not happy there just then.

Ten months before, when I was eighteen, I got married. I had married a handsome brown-skinned girl from Algiers, Louisiana, named Daisy Parker. We two kids should never have been married. We were too young to understand what it meant. I had to be up most of the night every night, playing in the orchestra, and in that way I neglected her, but I was so crazy about music that I couldn't think about much else. I see now it must have gone hard with a young and pretty girl up from a small town. And was she pretty! She naturally wanted to come ahead of everything else and she had a very high temper, partly, I guess, because she was so young and inexperienced. And in that same way I was quick to resent her remarks, so, as I say, we were not happy—in fact, we were very unhappy, both of us. . . .

Ory knew all about our troubles. He had done his best

to help smooth us out, but maybe nobody could have. So when he found I had the chance to go with that fine band on the river for a while, he understood it would be a good thing.

New Orleans, of course, was the hottest and gayest city on the Mississippi then, even including St. Louis, so all through the winter months, from November until April, when the weather is not so hot and New Orleans is at its highest, the excursion boats would stay right there, running dance excursions up and down the river every night and tying up in the daytime.

The steamer *Dixie Belle* was one of the biggest and best of them. She had her berth at the foot of Canal Street. The orchestra would start playing at eight o'clock while she was at the wharf, to attract people, and then she would shove out into the river at eight-thirty every night with a big crowd on board and cruise slowly around until about eleven o'clock when she would come back in. The *Dixie Belle* was fixed up inside something like a dance hall. She was a paddle wheeler, with great paddle wheels on each side, near the middle, and she had big open decks and could hold a lot of people.

So all that winter, which was the winter of 1919 and 1920, we cruised there around New Orleans and every night when we pulled in, of course I would go home to Daisy. Sometimes we were very happy, and I would hate to think of April coming, when I was to go north on the boat.

The orchestra on the *Dixie Belle* was . . . a twelve-piece orchestra and every man was a crackshot musician. "Fate" Marable had recruited them from the best bands in town, taking this man here and that one there and each one because he was a "hot" player on his own particular instrument. "Fate" was a fine swing pianist himself, and he knew that in time they would learn to play together. Now the most famous jazz orchestras of that day, as you will remember, had had no more than six or seven pieces (though some of the pure brass bands, the marching bands, had more). The old "Dixieland" had only five pieces, and so had Freddy Keppard's "Creole Band." "King" Oliver's famous "Magnolia" and Kid Ory's band had seven pieces each. So, you see, twelve pieces *was* big.

Winter passed and finally April came. The *Dixie Belle* was all cleaned out and fixed up with new paint and polish and finally the day came for us to start up the river. My mother and "Mamma Lucy" came down to see us off, but Daisy wasn't there. We had had another quarrel.

As we pulled out into the river and turned north, I began to feel funny, wishing one minute they'd left me back on the wharf and feeling keen the next moment that I was going. The sweeping of the paddle wheels got louder and louder as we got going. It seemed they had never made so much noise before—they were carrying me away from New Orleans for the first time.

In the seven months to come I was to follow the Mississippi for nearly two thousand miles, and visit many places. It was a handful of traveling, believe me, for a kid who'd always been afraid to leave home before.

We shoved away early in the morning so we could make Baton Rouge, our first stop, by night-down. It was a run of about eighty miles, upstream. A few passengers were on board, as it was to be a day trip, although the *Dixie Belle* was not meant to be a boat for regular passenger travel, but only for big excursion parties, so she was not fitted out with many staterooms.

It was a warm spring day and the river was high with water, but not flooding. The musicians did not have much to do except laze around on the decks and watch the shores, or now and then throw a little dice or something. After a while, when we had had our last look at New Orleans, I found myself a nice corner up on the top deck right under the pilot house and settled down with my trumpet and a polishing rag. I had bought myself a fine new instrument just before starting out, but even that wasn't shiny enough for *this* trip. No, suh! So I took the rag and shined her a little and then I put her to my mouth and tried out a few blasts. She sounded strong and sweet, with a good pure tone. I swung a little tune and saw we were going to get along fine together. So then I rubbed her up some more, taking my time, until I was satisfied. Over on the left shore a great cypress swamp was passing slowly by—there must have been hundreds of miles of it, stretching away off to the west—dark and hung all over with Spanish moss. I felt very happy where I was. The sun was just warm enough, the chunking of the paddle wheels was now pleasant to hear and everything was peaceful. Pretty soon I spread the rag on the deck beside me and lay my new trumpet on it and began to think of how lucky I really was. There I was, only nineteen years old, a member of a fine band, and starting out on my first big adventure. And I had my new trumpet to take with me. I reached over and let my hand lay on it, and felt very comfortable. . . .

LOUIS ARMSTRONG ON OLIVER

He would have been *big,* because there wasn't nobody doing nothing except Joe Oliver in those days. Bunk hadn't even been heard of; he was down there in the cotton fields wrestling with those bales, and forgot all about trumpet. They tried to get Joe to come to New York when he got hot, but he wouldn't come. And all the time the cats were coming out from New York with those big shows and picking up on what he was playing. Joe Oliver was *the* man in Chicago. But he came to New York too late. When he got there, everybody was playing him. Even I had been here long before him. And it was all his own fault, too, because he had Chicago sewed up. The agents and everybody coming from New York had wanted to bring him in someplace, *any* night club, with his band. But Joe wouldn't leave. "I'm doing all right here, man," he'd tell them. He had good jobs with good tips. So time ran out on him. He looked around, and when he came to New York—too late.

From then on he began to get what I guess you would call a broken heart. When you wind up playing with little old Musicians down in some place like Tampa, Florida, with cats that didn't even know him . . . And if you lay off for two days, the band breaks up. And the landlady commenced to hold his trunks. I saw him at that time; it was in Savannah, when I was on some one-nighters, and as far as I'm concerned that's what killed him—a broken heart. That's what killed Joe Oliver.

I was with him until they buried him; I was at his funeral. Most of the musicians turned out. The people who really knew him didn't forget him. It would have been nice if they'd had a parade for him, but instead they took him into the chapel across from the Lafayette—that big rehearsal hall in Harlem. I didn't like the sermon the preacher gave. Just because the Guild buried him was no reason for rubbing it in. They said he made money, and he had money, and didn't keep it. The Guild isn't supposed to say that; that's what we donate our services for when they give benefits. A lot of us didn't like that sermon, and even after all these years I still don't like to think about it.

He was a great man. I'll always remember him. But I don't care to remember him in Savannah, or the funeral. I'd rather think about a time like 1928, when I played two nights with Luis Russell's band at the Savoy, as a guest. Joe Oliver was there each night, with a new set of clothes, and that Panama hat like he usually wore. And he looked pleasant and happy. He was standing right in front of that trumpet. That was a thrill. I had run errands for his wife; he had brought me up to Chicago. And he stood there listening, with the tears coming right out of his eyes. It knocked me out.

I. Toward the Present

TALKING IT OVER

1. Why is it somehow fitting that Lily, the heroine of "The Lavender Evening Dress," should come back from the dead? Is there anything about her character that makes this, in its own way, plausible?

2. After reading the three New England anecdotes, what conclusions can you draw about the Yankee character?
   Analyze the New England sense of humor. What adjectives would you use to describe it?

3. Considering the poor odds, how do you account for the tremendous popularity of the "numbers game" in Harlem, as described in "The Hit"?

4. What aspects of Negro life are revealed in "The Barefoot Prophet" and "Sister Lucy"?

5. Discuss the attitudes of the speaker and the pawnbroker toward each other in "Pawnshop Blues."

6. Why does Simple feel that the country is not a fit place to live? Do you agree or disagree with his objections? Is the fact that Simple is a Negro in any way significant?

7. Why has Babe Ruth become a legend, while so many other fine baseball players of the past have not? Can you compare him to any of the heroes in Part Four?

8. Why was Joe Oliver a tragic figure, according to Louis Armstrong?

ON YOUR OWN

If you would like to know more about the New England character, you might enjoy reading the following selections:

1. The poems of Robert Frost, particularly "Mending Wall," "The Death of the Hired Man," "Two Tramps in Mud-Time," "After Apple-Picking," "Home Burial," "The Investment."

2. The short stories of Sarah Orne Jewett, which take place along the Maine coast.

3. "Mr. Flood's Party" and "New England," two poems by Edward Arlington Robinson.

4. *New England Folklore*, by B. A. Botkin.

A vast selection of the folk literature of the American Negro can be found in *Negro Folklore*, edited by Langston Hughes and Arna Bontemps.

II

The Beginnings

The earliest American folklore belonged, of course, to the Indian. For an unknown number of years before the coming of the white man to the present, each tribe preserved its own stories, myths, legends, songs, and religious rituals. These survived mainly because the Indian, even today, has remained apart from the mainstream of American culture.

Plantation Negroes developed their own folklore for much the same reason. Largely illiterate and denied access to the white culture, they began an oral tradition which owed very little to the white man. The animal tales in this chapter were based on African folk tradition, but they were adapted to fit a new and frightening situation. Brer Rabbit, the hero of many of these tales, represented the slave. Like him, the rabbit was helpless against his stronger fellow creatures. The slaves, however, invested this timid animal with cunning, which enabled him to outwit sly Brer Fox and stupid Brer Bear and thus preserve his life. These stories provided humor and moral instruction for the Negro, but more important, they emphasized to him that a powerful adversary could be defeated through shrewdness and imagination.

The third group represented here are the pre-Revolutionary Dutch. Their literary and folk traditions came from Europe, but they often created new material to fit the strange new land they had come to colonize. Taken together, these three traditions offer the reader an idea of the earliest American folklore.

Two Ojibwa Tales

The author of the following two stories married an Ojibwa princess, and their marriage gave him access to many tales and legends of her tribe. These stories remind the reader of the early Indian's closeness to nature, and his lack of distinction between the natural and supernatural.

THE WHITE STONE CANOE

by Henry Rowe Schoolcraft

There was once a very beautiful young girl, who died suddenly on the day she was to have been married to a handsome young man. He was also brave, but his heart was not proof against this loss. From the hour she was buried, there was no more joy or peace for him. He went often to visit the spot where the women had buried her, and sat musing there, when it was thought, by some of his friends, he would have done better to try to amuse himself in the chase, or by diverting his thought in the warpath. But war and hunting had both lost their charms for him. His heart was already dead within him. He pushed aside both his war club and his bow and arrows.

He had heard the old people say that there was a path that led to the land of souls, and he determined to follow it. He accordingly set out, one morning, after having completed his preparations for the journey. At first he hardly knew which way to go. He was only guided by the tradition that he must go south. For a while he could see no change in the face of the country. Forests, and hills, and valleys, and streams had the same looks which they wore in his native place. There

was snow on the ground, when he set out, and it was sometimes seen to be piled and matted on the thick trees and
bushes. At length it began to diminish, and finally disappeared. The forest assumed a more cheerful appearance, and
the leaves put forth their buds, and before he was aware of
the completeness of the change, he found himself surrounded
by spring. He had left behind him the land of snow and ice.
The air became mild; the dark clouds of winter had rolled
away from the sky; a pure field of blue was above him, and
as he went he saw flowers beside his path, and heard the
songs of birds. By these signs he knew that he was going the
right way, for they agreed with the traditions of his tribe. At
length he spied a path. It led him through a grove, then up a
long and elevated ridge, on the very top of which he came to
a lodge. At the door stood an old man, with white hair whose
eyes though deeply sunk, had a fiery brilliancy. He had a
long robe of skins thrown loosely around his shoulders, and
a staff in his hands. It was Chebiabos.

The young Chippewa began to tell his story; but the
venerable chief arrested him, before he had proceeded to
speak ten words. "I have expected you," he replied, "and had
just risen to bid you welcome to my abode. She whom you
seek, passed here but a few days since, and being fatigued
with her journey, rested herself here. Enter my lodge and be
seated, and I will then satisfy your inquiries, and give you
directions for your journey from this point." Having done
this, they both issued forth to the lodge door. "You see yon-
der gulf," said he, "and the wide stretching blue plains beyond. It is the land of souls. You stand upon its borders, and
my lodge is the gate of entrance. But you cannot take your
body along. Leave it here with your bow and arrows, your
bundle, and your dog. You will find them safe on your return."
So saying, he re-entered the lodge and the freed traveller
bounded forward, as if his feet had suddenly been endowed
with the power of wings. But all things retained their natural

colors and shapes. The woods and leaves, and streams and lakes, were only more bright and comely than he had ever witnessed. Animals bounded across his path, with a freedom and a confidence which seemed to tell him, there was no blood shed here. Birds of beautiful plumage inhabited the groves, and sported in the waters. There was but one thing, in which he saw a very unusual effect. He noticed that his passage was not stopped by trees or other objects. He appeared to walk directly through them. They were, in fact, but the souls or shadows of material trees. He became sensible that he was in a land of shadows. When he had travelled half a day's journey, through a country which was continually becoming more attractive, he came to the banks of a broad lake, in the centre of which was a large and beautiful island. He found a canoe of shining white stone, tied to the shore. He was now sure that he had come the right path, for the aged man had told him of this. There were also shining paddles. He immediately entered the canoe, and took the paddles in his hands, when to his joy and surprise, on turning round, he beheld the object of his search in another canoe, exactly its counterpart in everything. She had exactly imitated his motions, and they were side by side. They at once pushed out from shore and began to cross the lake. Its waves seemed to be rising, and at a distance looked ready to swallow them up; but just as they entered the whitened edge of them they seemed to melt away, as if they were but the images of waves. But no sooner was one wreath of foam passed, than another, more threatening still, rose up. Thus they were in perpetual fear; and what added to it, was the clearness of the water, through which they could see heaps of beings who had perished before, and whose bones lay strewed on the bottom of the lake. The Master of Life had, however, decreed to let them pass, for the actions of neither of them had been bad. But they saw many others struggling and sinking in the waves. Old men and young men, males and females of all ages and ranks, were there; some passed, and some sank. It was only the little children whose canoes seemed to meet no waves. At length, every difficulty was gone, as in a moment, and they both leaped out on the happy island. They felt that the very air was food. It strengthened and nourished them. They wandered together over the blissful fields, where everything was formed to please the eye and the ear. There were no tempests—there was no ice, no chilly winds—no one shivered for the want of warm clothes: no one suffered for hunger—no one mourned the dead. They saw no graves. They heard of no wars. There was no hunting of animals; for the air itself was their food. Gladly would the young warrior have remained there forever, but he was obliged to go back for his body. He did not see the Master of Life, but he heard his voice in a soft breeze. "Go back," said this voice, "to the land from whence you come. Your time has not yet come. The duties for which I made you, and which you are to perform, are not yet finished. Return to your people and accomplish the duties of a good man. You will be the ruler of your tribe for many days. The rules you must observe will be told you by my messenger, who keeps the gate. When he surrenders back your body, he will tell you what to do. Listen to him, and you shall afterwards rejoin the spirit, which you must now leave behind. She is accepted, and will be ever here, as young and as happy as she was when I first called her from the land of snows." When this voice ceased, the narrator awoke. It was the fancy work of a dream, and he was still in the bitter land of snows, and hunger, and tears.

MONDAWMIN; OR,
THE ORIGIN OF INDIAN CORN
by Henry Rowe Schoolcraft

In times past, a poor Indian was living with his wife and children in a beautiful part of the country. He was not only poor, but inexpert in procuring food for his family, and his children were all too young to give him assistance. Although poor, he was a man of a kind and contented disposition. He was always thankful to the Great Spirit for everything he received. The same disposition was inherited by his eldest son, who had now arrived at the proper age to undertake the ceremony of the Ke-ig-uish-im-o-win, or fast, to see what kind of a spirit would be his guide and guardian through life. Wunzh, for this was his name, had been an obedient boy from his infancy, and was of a pensive, thoughtful, and mild disposition, so that he was beloved by the whole family. As soon as the first indications of spring appeared, they built him the customary little lodge at a retired spot, some distance from their own, where he would not be disturbed during this solemn rite. In the mean time he prepared himself, and immediately went into it, and commenced his fast. The first few days, he amused himself, in the morning, by walking in the woods and over the mountains, examining the early plants and flowers, and in this way prepared himself to enjoy his sleep, and, at the same time, stored his mind with pleasant ideas for his dreams. While he rambled through the woods, he felt a strong desire to know how the plants, herbs, and berries grew, without any aid from man, and why it was that some species were good to eat, and others possessed medicinal or poisonous juices. He recalled these thoughts to mind after he became too languid to walk about, and had confined himself strictly to the lodge; he wished he could dream of something that would prove a benefit to his father and family, and to all others. "True!" he thought, "the Great Spirit made all things, and it is to him that we owe our lives. But could he not make it easier for us to get our food, than by hunting animals and taking fish? I must try to find out this in my visions."

On the third day he became weak and faint, and kept his bed. He fancied, while thus lying, that he saw a handsome young man coming down from the sky and advancing towards him. He was richly and gayly dressed, having on a great many garments of green and yellow colors, but differing in their deeper or lighter shades. He had a plume of waving feathers on his head, and all his motions were graceful.

"I am sent to you, my friend," said the celestial visitor, "by that Great Spirit who made all things in the sky and on the earth. He has seen and knows your motives in fasting. He sees that it is from a kind and benevolent wish to do good to your people, and to procure a benefit for them, and that you do not seek for strength in war or the praise of warriors. I am sent to instruct you, and show you how you can do your kindred good." He then told the young man to arise, and prepare to wrestle with him, as it was only by this means that he could hope to succeed in his wishes. Wunzh knew he was weak from fasting, but he felt his courage rising in his heart, and immediately got up, determined to die rather than fail. He commenced the trial, and after a protracted effort, was almost exhausted, when the beautiful stranger said, "My friend, it is enough for once; I will come again to try you"; and, smiling on him, he ascended in the air in the same direction from which he came. The next day the celestial visitor reappeared at the same hour and renewed the trial. Wunzh felt that his strength was even less than the day before, but the courage of his mind seemed to increase in proportion as his body became weaker. Seeing this, the stranger again spoke to him in the same words he used before, adding, "Tomorrow will be your last trial. Be strong, my friend, for this is the only way you can overcome me, and obtain the boon you seek." On the third day he again appeared at the same time and renewed the struggle. The poor youth was very faint in body, but grew stronger in mind at every contest, and was determined to prevail or perish in the attempt. He exerted his utmost powers, and after the contest had been continued the usual time, the stranger ceased his efforts and declared himself conquered. For the first time he entered the lodge, and sitting down beside the youth, he began to deliver his instructions to him, telling him in what manner he should proceed to take advantage of his victory.

"You have won your desires of the Great Spirit," said the stranger. "You have wrestled manfully. Tomorrow will be the seventh day of your fasting. Your father will give you food to strengthen you, and as it is the last day of trial, you will prevail. I know this, and now tell you what you must do to benefit your family and your tribe. Tomorrow," he repeated, "I shall meet you and wrestle with you for the last time; and, as soon as you have prevailed against me, you will strip off my garments and throw me down, clean the earth of roots and weeds, make it soft, and bury me in the spot. When you have done this, leave my body in the earth, and do not disturb it, but come occasionally to visit the place, to see whether I have come to life, and be careful never to let the grass or weeds grow on my grave. Once a month cover me with fresh earth. If you follow my instructions, you will accomplish your object of doing good to your fellow-creatures by teaching them the knowledge I now teach you." He then shook him by the hand and disappeared.

In the morning the youth's father came with some slight refreshments, saying, "My son, you have fasted long enough. If the Great Spirit will favor you, he will do it now. It is seven days since you have tasted food, and you must not sacrifice your life. The Master of Life does not require that." "My father," replied the youth, "wait till the sun goes down. I have a particular reason for extending my fast to that hour." "Very well," said the old man, "I shall wait till the hour arrives, and you feel inclined to eat."

At the usual hour of the day the sky visitor returned, and the trial of strength was renewed. Although the youth had not availed himself of his father's offer of food, he felt that new strength had been given to him, and that exertion had renewed his strength and fortified his courage. He grasped his angelic antagonist with supernatural strength, threw him down, took from him his beautiful garments and plume, and finding him dead, immediately buried him on the spot, taking all the precautions he had been told of, and being very confident, at the same time, that his friend would again come to life. He then returned to his father's lodge, and partook sparingly of the meal that had been prepared for him. But he never for a moment forgot the grave of his friend. He carefully visited it throughout the spring, and weeded out the grass, and kept the ground in a soft and pliant state. Very soon he saw the tops of the green plumes coming through the ground; and the more careful he was to obey his instructions in keeping the ground in order, the faster they grew. He was, however, careful to conceal the exploit from his father. Days and weeks had passed in this way. The summer was now drawing towards a close, when one day, after a long absence in hunting, Wunzh invited his father to follow him to the quiet and lonesome spot of his former fast. The lodge had been removed, and the weeds kept from growing on the circle where it stood, but in its place stood a tall and graceful plant, with bright-colored silken hair, surmounted with nodding plumes and stately leaves, and golden clusters on each side. "It is my friend," shouted the lad; "it is the friend of all mankind. It is Mondawmin. We need no longer rely on hunting alone; for, as long as this gift is cherished and taken care of, the ground itself will give us a living." He then pulled an ear. "See, my father," said he, "this is what I fasted for. The Great Spirit has listened to my voice, and sent us something new, and henceforth our people will not alone depend upon the chase or upon the waters."

He then communicated to his father the instructions given him by the stranger. He told him that the broad husks must be torn away, as he had pulled off the garments in his wrestling; and having done this, directed him how the ear must be held before the fire till the outer skin became brown, while all the milk was retained in the grain. The whole family then united in a feast on the newly grown ears, expressing gratitude to the Merciful Spirit who gave it. So corn came into the world.

THE ORIGIN OF FIRE[1]
by Ella E. Clark

This Nez Percé tale relates how mankind received the price-less gift of fire from the heavens.

Long ago the Nimipu had no fire. They could see fire in the sky sometimes, but it belonged to the Great Power. He kept it in great black bags in the sky. When the bags bumped into each other, there was a crashing, tearing sound, and through the hole that was made fire sparkled.

People longed to get it. They ate fish and meat raw as the animals do. They ate roots and berries raw as the bears do. The women grieved when they saw their little ones shivering and blue with cold. The medicine men beat on their drums in their efforts to bring fire down from the sky, but no fire came.

At last a boy just beyond the age for the sacred vigil said that he would get the fire. People laughed at him. The medicine men angrily complained, "Do you think that you can do what we are not able to do?"

But the boy went on and made his plans. The first time that he saw the black fire bags drifting in the sky, he got

[1]Reprinted by permission from *Indian Legends from the Northern Rockies*, by Ella E. Clark, copyright 1966 by the University of Oklahoma Press.

ready. First he bathed, brushing himself with fir branches until he was entirely clean and was fragrant with the smell of fir. He looked very handsome.

With the inside bark of cedar he wrapped an arrowhead and placed it beside his best and largest bow. On the ground he placed a beautiful white shell that he often wore around his neck. Then he asked his guardian spirit to help him reach the cloud with his arrow.

All the people stood watching. The medicine men said among themselves, "Let us have him killed, lest he make the Great Power angry."

But the people said, "Let him alone. Perhaps he can bring the fire down. If he does not, then we can kill him."

The boy waited until he saw that the largest fire bag was over his head, growling and rumbling. Then he raised his bow and shot the arrow straight upward. Suddenly, all the people heard a tremendous crash, and they saw a flash of fire in the sky. Then the burning arrow, like a falling star, came hurtling down among them. It struck the boy's white shell and there made a small flame.

Shouting with joy, the people rushed forward. They lighted sticks and dry bark and hurried to their tipis to start fires with them. Children and old people ran around, laughing and singing.

When the excitement had died down, people asked about the boy. But he was nowhere to be seen. On the ground lay his shell, burned so that it showed the fire colors. Near it lay the boy's bow. People tried to shoot with it, but not even the strongest man and best with bow and arrow could bend it.

The boy was never seen again. But his abalone shell is still beautiful, still touched with the colors of flame. And the fire he brought from the black bag is still in the center of each tipi, the blessing of every home.

CHIEF CLIFF[2]
by Ella E. Clark

This Kutenai legend, told by Pat Shea, a U.S. Forest Service employee on the Flathead Reservation, reveals the high esteem felt by Indians for a noble death.

Years ago, an aged chief of the Kutenais felt that he no longer had control of his band. In his younger years he had done many deeds of bravery and many acts of generosity, but now the young men in his band did not care to hear about them. He had laid down rules of conduct which were for the betterment of his people, but the young men and women now gave no heed to them.

They were fast departing from the ways of their elders and were following the wishes and the orders of a subchief. Much younger than the old chief, this man would probably be head man when the chief died. But he, too, was not in sympathy with the old ways, and he seldom counseled with his elders.

The old chief was sick at heart because of the changing ways and because of the young people's neglect of him. What could he do to regain the respect of his band? What could he do to remind them of his former bravery and prowess?

One summer when his people were camped at the base of the high, steep cliff north of Elmo, he thought of the answer to his questions. While the others were making merry with games and dancing, he planned how he would once more prove his worth. He dressed himself in his finest buckskin and in the headdress which showed his deeds in war. He

[2]Reprinted by permission from *Indian Legends from the Northern Rockies,* by Ella E. Clark, copyright 1966 by the University of Oklahoma Press.

arrayed his favorite horse in a richly decorated saddle blanket and put on him his best buckskin saddle.

Then he mounted his horse and, sitting erect and proud, rode to the top of the ridge and along its crest to the edge of the cliff. Seeing him up there, everyone in the camp stopped his work or his play and watched in wonder. Why was he dressed in ceremonial garb? What had caused the change in his bearing?

When all were looking up at him in silence, the old man began to address them in the strong tones of his younger years: "Hear me, my people. My heart is heavy with grief because you have forgotten the teachings of your elders. You have forgotten their brave deeds and their generous acts: The stories about them—stories which have been handed down for generations as examples for young people to follow—you now pay no attention to. Soon they will be forgotten.

"Only ill luck and misery will come to those who forsake the laws and the teachings of the elders of the tribe. Knowing that, I will make one last effort to remind you of the bravery and the wisdom of your grandfathers."

When he had finished speaking, he turned his horse and rode slowly back along the ridge. Suddenly he wheeled round, tightened the reins, and urged the horse at full speed back toward the cliff. In wonder and then in horror, the people below watched him, noting that he was singing the death chant. Still chanting, he rode on beyond the edge of the cliff. Horse and rider turned over and over among the rocks at the foot of the ridge.

All the people hurried to the spot. The women began the death wail. Sadly the men disentangled the body from the saddle and the horse's trappings. Some prepared it for burial, while others looked for the best place for the grave of the old chief. As it was already late afternoon, burial would not be until morning.

That evening there were no games or gambling or laughter around the camp fires. All spoke in subdued tones or listened in silence to the old men of the tribe. One after another they arose and paid tribute to their dead leader. Some spoke about his prowess in war, when they had been attacked by the enemy and he had led them as a war chief.

Some spoke of his kindness to the poor of the tribe. "When there was food," they recalled, "he always saw to it that no one was hungry. The good of all his people was near and dear to his heart. Like a good chief, he was generous as well as brave. And he always obeyed the laws of the tribe."

The young men and young women, the boys and girls, all listened with pride in their hearts. "He was a greater chief than we knew," they said among themselves.

"It is well for us to respect the old people for what they have done," the young people said. "We must not overlook any of the old ones. We, too, will be old some day. We will remember the brave deed and the wise counsel of the good chief. The cliff will always remind us of him."

That is why the cliff is called Chief Cliff. And that is why the Kutenais, ever since, have remembered to treat their old people with kindness and with honor.

Early Negro Stories

These three early Negro stories are fables, or tales in which animals talk and act like human beings. A successful fable, as you will see here, teaches a lesson in an amusing and painless manner.

BRER FOX AND THE GOOBERS

by Carl Carmer

Brer Rabbit seen Brer B'ar one day a'settin' out to dig goobers wid de donkey draggin' de dump cart. Brer Rabbit say me an' Miss Rabbit an' all them little rabbits sho' is hungry fo goobers. So he go home an' fin' him a red string an' tie it 'roun' his neck an' he run an' lay down in de road where Brer B'ar would be com'n by wid de cart carryin' his sack filled up wid goobers.

By'n by Brer B'ar come along an' de donkey shy so he 'most upset de cart. Brer B'ar git out an' he say: "If'n it ain't Brer Rabbit as dead as a doornail wid his throat cut. Make good rabbit stew foh me an' Miss B'ar." So he pick up Brer Rabbit an' fling him in de cart an' go on. Soon's his back is turned Brer Rabbit fling out de bag o' goobers an' jump out heself an' run home. On de way he meet Brer Fox an' Brer Fox say: "Where you git dat bag o' goobers?" an' Brer Rabbit tell him.

Soon's Brer B'ar come in sight er his house, way behime dem dark pines, he holler to his ole 'oman:

"Hello dar. Come heah, Miss B'ar:
Goobers heah; rabbits dar!"

Miss B'ar she run out de cabin. She run 'roun' de dump cart. She look in. Des a lil' rattlin' load o' goobers in de bottom er de cart. She say:

"Goobers gone, rabbit gone, bag gone!"

Brer B'ar tu'n 'roun' an' look, he scratched his head, he say: "Dat 'ar rabbit done left me bar."

Next day he hitch up de donkey to de dump cart an' start to de patch to haul up mo' goobers. His ole 'oman, she tell him: "Watch out, don' drap noddin' on de big road wid dis nex' load."

Dis time Brer Fox he 'low he'll git his winter's pervisions by speculatin' wid Brer B'ar's load, labor and land.

Brer Fox git a red string, he do. He tie hit 'roun' his neck. He go to de big road. Same place what Brer Rabbit done lay down, Brer Fox he done lay down. He keep des' as still. D'reckly heah come Brer B'ar wid 'noder heapin' load o' goobers.

De donkey he shy agin at de same place. Brer B'ar he git off de cart, he look at Brer Fox, he say: "What dis mean? Un-hum! Maybe perhaps de same thief what stole my goobers yestiddy. You got de same like red 'roun' your th'oat. Maybe perhaps you dead too. He feel Brer Fox, he say: "You good weight too, I take you to my ole 'oman, maybe you'll make er good stew."

Wid dat Brer Fox think he sho' goin' git good chance to git his fill er goobers.

Brer B'ar he lif' Brer Fox by de behime legs, he say:

"Maybe you be dead, er maybe no,
But I will make you dead for sho'!"

And wid dat he swing Brer Fox 'roun' and lam his head 'ginst de wheel er de cart.

Dat lick like to kilt Brer Fox. Hit all he can do to jerk his behime legs loose from Brer B'ar and run home t'rough de dark pines. He had de swole head some seasons frum dat lick. Chillum, de same cunnin' trick ain't apt to work twict.

THE FOX AND THE GOOSE

One day a Fox was going down the road and saw a Goose. "Good-morning, Goose," he said; and the Goose flew up on a limb and said, "Good-morning, Fox."

Then the Fox said, "You ain't afraid of me, is you? Haven't you heard of the meeting up at the hall the other night?"

"No, Fox. What was that?"

"You haven't heard about all the animals meeting up at the hall! Why, they passed a law that no animal must hurt any other animal. Come down and let me tell you about it. The hawk mustn't catch the chicken, and the dog mustn't chase the rabbit, and the lion mustn't hurt the lamb. No animal must hurt any other animal."

"Is that so!"

"Yes, all live friendly together. Come down, and don't be afraid."

As the Goose was about to fly down, way off in the woods they heard a "Woo-wooh! woo-wooh!" and the Fox looked around.

"Come down, Goose," he said.

And the Dog got closer. "Woo-wooh!"

Then the Fox started to sneak off; and the Goose said, "Fox, you ain't scared of the Dog, is you? Didn't all the animals pass a law at the meeting not to bother each other any more?"

"Yes," replied the Fox as he trotted away quickly, "the animals passed the law; but some of the animals round here ain't got much respec' for the law."

OLE SIS GOOSE

by W. A. Eddins

Ole Sis Goose wus er-sailin' on de lake, and ole Br'er Fox wus hid in de weeds. By um by ole Sis Goose swum up close to der bank and ole Br'er Fox lept out an cotched her.

"O yes, ole Sis Goose, I'se got yer now, you'se been er-sailin' on der lake er long time, en I'se got yer now. I'se gwine to break yer neck en pick yer bones."

"Hole on der', Br'er Fox, hold on, I'se got jes' as much right to swim in der lake as you has ter lie in der weeds. Hit's jes' as much my lake es hit is yours, and we is gwine to take dis matter to der cotehouse and see if you has any right to break my neck and pick my bones."

And so dey went to cote, and when dey got dere, de sheriff, he wus er fox, en de judge, he wus er fox, and der tourneys, dey wus fox, en all de jurymen, dey was foxes, too.

En dey tried ole Sis Goose en dey 'victed her and dey 'scuted her, and dey picked her bones.

Now, my chilluns, listen to me, when all de folks in de cotehouse is foxes, and you is des' er common goose, der ain't gwine to be much jestice for you pore cullud folks.

WHY SPUYTEN DUYVIL IS SO NAMED

by Charles M. Skinner

This mock-heroic tale commemorates the courage of a Dutch trumpeter attacked by the Devil.

The tidewater creek that forms the upper boundary of Manhattan Island is known to dwellers in tenements round about as "Spittin' Divvle." The proper name of it is Spuyten Duyvil, and this, in turn, is the compression of a celebrated boast by Anthony Van Corlaer. This redoubtable gentleman, famous for fat, long wind, and long whiskers, was trumpeter for the garrison at New Amsterdam, which his countryman had just bought for twenty-four dollars, and he sounded the brass so sturdily that in the fight between the Dutch and Indians at the Dey Street peach orchard his blasts struck more terror into the red men's hearts than did the matchlocks of his comrades. William the Testy vowed that Anthony and his trumpet were garrison enough for all Manhattan Island, for he argued that no regiment of Yankees would approach near enough to be struck with lasting deafness, as must have happened if they came when Anthony was awake.

Peter Stuyvesant—Peter the Headstrong—showed his appreciation of Anthony's worth by making him his esquire, and when he got news of an English expedition on its way to seize his unoffending colony, he at once ordered Anthony to rouse the villages along the Hudson with a trumpet call to war. The esquire took a hurried leave of six or eight ladies, each of whom delighted to believe that his affections were lavished on her alone, and bravely started northward, his trumpet hanging on one side, a stone bottle, much heavier, depending from the other. It was a stormy evening when he arrived at the upper end of the island, and there was no ferryman in sight, so, after fuming up and down the shore, he swallowed a mighty draught of Dutch courage—for he was as accomplished a performer on the horn as on the trumpet—and swore with ornate and voluminous oaths that he would swim the stream "in spite of the devil" [En spuyt den Duyvil].

He plunged in, and had gone half-way across when the Evil One, not to be spited, appeared as a huge moss bunker, vomiting boiling water and lashing a fiery tail. This dreadful fish seized Anthony by the leg; but the trumpeter was game, for, raising his instrument to his lips, he exhaled his last breath through it in a defiant blast that rang through the woods for miles and made the devil himself let go for a moment. Then he was dragged below, his nose shining through the water more and more faintly, until, at last, all sight of him was lost. The failure of his mission resulted in the downfall of the Dutch in America, for, soon after, the English won a bloodless victory, and St. George's cross flaunted from the ramparts where Anthony had so often saluted the setting sun. But it was years, even then, before he was hushed, for in stormy weather it was claimed that the shrill of his trumpet could be heard near the creek that he had named, sounding above the deeper roar of the blast.

II. The Beginnings

TALKING IT OVER

1. a) The theme of a journey is a popular one in literature. In "The White Stone Canoe," the journey is to another world. Discuss what the youth discovered about the other world and how it differed from his own.
   b) How did the Indian and his lover manage to cross the lake when so many others failed? Who else was permitted to cross? Why? What religious beliefs are implicit in these occurrences?

2. a) After reading "Mondawmin," what conclusions can you draw about the religious beliefs of these Indians? What was their concept of God and his role in man's life?
   b) Why do you suppose Wunzh was made to wrestle with the young man for four days before he was given the secret of how to raise corn? Why was this trial necessary?

3. Why were the medicine men in "The Origin of Fire" disturbed—and angry—when the boy was preparing to bring the fire to earth? Does this element in human nature still exist today?

4. Both "Mondawmin" and "The Origin of Fire" explained the origin of certain natural phenomena—corn and fire. Why do you think myths of this type evolved and were passed down from generation to generation? What function did they serve?

5. a) Do you think the old chief's act was heroic? If so, what did he hope to achieve? Did he succeed?

b) Does this story have contemporary significance in what it has to say about the "generation gap"?

6. a) "Brer Fox and the Goobers," "The Fox and the Goose," and "Ole Sis Goose" are didactic folk tales; that is, they are intended to teach a moral. Discuss the lesson stated by each, and how it is presented in the tale.

   b) Is the lesson of "Ole Sis Goose" relevant today?

7. How does the tone of "Why Spuyten Duyvil Is So Named" make this story different from other tales about folk heroes? What is the author's attitude toward Anthony Van Corlaer?

ON YOUR OWN

1. Compare "The Origin of Fire" with the Greek myth of Prometheus, the fire-bringer, as retold in Edith Hamilton's *Mythology*. For a more modern treatment, you may enjoy reading *Anthem*, a short novel by Ayn Rand.

2. The device of the animal story used to point out a moral is not a new one in literature. You may want to compare the three fables in this chapter to those of Aesop, or to "The Nun's Priest's Tale" in *The Canterbury Tales*, by Chaucer, in which a fox is also the main character. For modern variations of this ancient literary form, read *Fables for Our Time*, by James Thurber, and *Animal Farm*, by George Orwell.

3. The story of Anthony Van Corlaer can also be found, along with other tales of the Dutch in America, in *Knickerbocker's History of New York*, by Washington Irving. Van Corlaer's comic death is described in Book VII, Chapter X.

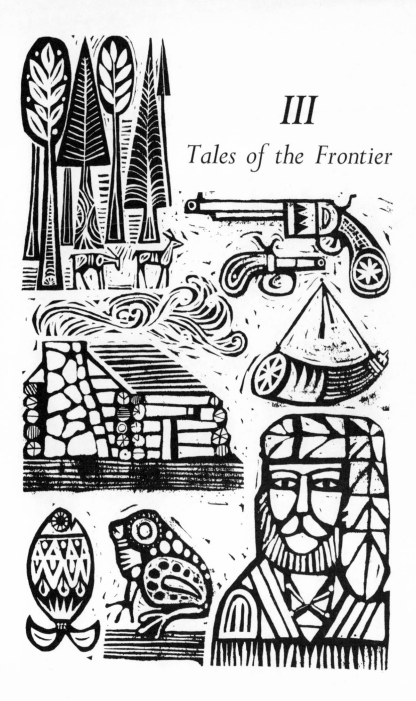

III

Tales of the Frontier

Life on the frontier was different from anything we will ever experience again. Danger was plentiful, hardships were ever-present, and the basic conveniences of civilization, including law and order, were absent. It is not surprising that frontier folklore should be extravagant, full of wild exaggerations and incredible heroes. If nature could produce vast mountain ranges, endless forests, and countless herds of buffalo, man was not to be outdone. To cope with this awesome environment, the frontiersman had to be much larger than life, and so was his imagination. If Davy Crockett in real life was not quite a god, the stories by and about him soon made him one. If Wyatt Earp did not really shoot down hundreds of gunfighters in face-to-face confrontations, folklore said that he did, and civilized America believed it.

Today we like our heroes scaled to human size. Man has become a good deal smaller since the days of the frontier, and we may be poorer for it. But the legends of the frontier, farfetched though they may be to our critical age, still stir a sympathetic chord in our imaginations. Through them, we may leave our secure, mechanized, complex era and return to a more innocent time.

THE JUMPING FROG

from the Sonora *Herald,* June 11, 1853

This is the earliest known printed version of a popular California folk tale. It appeared in the Sonora Herald *of June 11, 1853. Mark Twain's version, which follows, shows how a gift-*

*ed storyteller can transform rather unpromising material into
a classic tall tale.*

A toad story.—A long stupid-looking fellow used to frequent a gambling saloon, some time since, and was in the
habit of promenading up and down, but never speaking. The
boys began to play with him, at last, and in down east drawl
he gave them Rolands for their Olivers till they left him alone.
At night he spread out his blankets on an empty monte table
and lived like a gambler, except that he talked to no one nor
gambled a cent. He became at length, an acknowledged character, slunk in and out, and the boys tittered as they saw him
pass. One day he came in with an important air, and said:

"I have got a toad that'll leap further than any toad you
can scare up."

They soon surrounded him, and roared and laughed.

"Yes," says he, "I'll bet money on it. Barkeeper, give me
a cigar box to hold my toad in."

The fun was great, and the oddity was the talk of all
hands. A gambler, in the evening, happened to come across
a big frog, fetched him to the gaming house and offered to
jump him against the Yankee's toad.

"Well," says Yank, "I'll bet liquors on it." A chalk line
was made and the toad put down. They struck the boards behind the toad and he leaped six feet, then the frog leaped
seven. Yank paid the liquors; but next morning, he says aloud:

"My toad waren't beat. No man's toad can leap with my
toad. I have two ounces and two double eagles, and all of
them I bet on my toad." The boys bet with him again, and
his toad leaped six feet, but the frog leaped only two feet.

"The best two out of three," said the gamblers.

"Very well," says Yank. But still the frog could not go
over two feet. Yank pocketed the bets.

"My frog is darn heavy this morning," says the gambler.

"I reckoned it would be, stranger," says the Yankee, "for I rolled a pound of shot into him last night."

THE CELEBRATED JUMPING FROG OF CALAVERAS COUNTY

by Samuel Langhorne Clemens (Mark Twain)

In compliance with the request of a friend of mine, who wrote me from the East, I called on good-natured, garrulous old Simon Wheeler, and inquired after my friend's friend, *Leonidas W.* Smiley, as requested to do, and I hereunto append the result. I have a lurking suspicion that *Leonidas W.* Smiley is a myth; that my friend never knew such a personage; and that he only conjectured that, if I asked old Wheeler about him, it would remind him of his infamous *Jim* Smiley, and he would go to work and bore me nearly to death with some infernal reminiscence of him as long and tedious as it should be useless to me. If that was the design, it certainly succeeded.

I found Simon Wheeler dozing comfortably by the barroom stove of the old, dilapidated tavern in the ancient mining camp of Angel's, and I noticed that he was fat and baldheaded, and had an expression of winning gentleness and simplicity upon his tranquil countenance. He roused up and gave me good-day. I told him a friend of mine had commissioned me to make some inquiries about a cherished companion of his boyhood named *Leonidas W.* Smiley—*Rev. Leonidas W.* Smiley—a young minister of the Gospel, who he had heard was at one time a resident of Angel's Camp. I added that, if Mr. Wheeler could tell me anything about this Rev. Leonidas W. Smiley, I would feel under many obligations to him.

Simon Wheeler backed me into a corner and blockaded me there with his chair, and then sat me down and reeled off the monotonous narrative which follows this paragraph. He never smiled, he never frowned, he never changed his voice from the gentle-flowing key to which he tuned the initial sentence, he never betrayed the slightest suspicion of enthusiasm; but all through the interminable narrative there ran a vein of impressive earnestness and sincerity, which showed me plainly that, so far from his imagining that there was anything ridiculous or funny about his story, he regarded it as a really important matter, and admired its two heroes as men of transcendent genius in *finesse*. To me, the spectacle of a man drifting serenely along through such a queer yarn without ever smiling, was exquisitely absurd. As I said before, I asked him to tell me what he knew of Rev. Leonidas W. Smiley, and he replied as follows. I let him go on in his own way, and never interrupted him once:

There was a feller here once by the name of *Jim* Smiley, in the winter of '49—or may be it was the spring of '50— I don't recollect exactly, somehow, though what makes me think it was one or the other is because I remember the big flume wasn't finished when he first came to the camp; but any way, he was the curiosest man about always betting on any thing that turned up you ever see, if he could get any body to bet on the other side; and if he couldn't, he'd change sides. Any way that suited the other man would suit him—any way just so's he got a bet, *he* was satisfied. But still he was lucky, uncommon lucky; he most always come out winner. He was always ready and laying for a chance; there couldn't be no solit'ry thing mentioned but that feller'd offer to bet on it, and take any side you please, as I was just telling you. If there was a horse-race, you'd find him flush, or you'd find him busted at the end of it; if there was a dog-fight, he'd bet on it; if there was a chicken-fight, he'd bet on it; why, if there was two birds setting on a fence, he would bet you which one would fly first; or if there was a camp-meeting, he would be there reg'lar, to bet on Parson Walker, which he judged to be the best exhorter about there, and so he was, too, and a good man. If he even seen a straddle-bug start to go anywheres, he would bet you how long it would take him to get wherever he was going to, and if you took him up, he would foller that straddle-bug to Mexico but what he would find out where he was bound for and how long he was on the road. Lots of the boys here has seen that Smiley, and can tell you about him. Why, it never made no difference to him—he would bet on *any* thing—the dangdest feller. Parson Walker's wife laid very sick once, for a good while, and it seemed as if they warn't going to save her; but one morning he come in, and Smiley asked how she was, and he said she was considerable better— thank the Lord for his inf'nite mercy—and coming on so smart that, with the blessing of Prov'dence, she'd get well yet; and Smiley, before he thought, says, "Well, I'll resk two-and-a-half that she don't, anyway."

Thish-yer Smiley had a mare—the boys called her the fifteen-minute nag, but that was only in fun, you know, because, of course, she was faster than that—and he used to win money on that horse, for all she was so slow and always had the asthma, or the distemper, or the consumption, or something of that kind. They used to give her two or three hundred yards start, and then pass her under way; but always at the fag end of the race she'd get excited and desperate-like, and come cavorting and straddling up, and scattering her legs around limber, sometimes in the air, and sometimes out to one side amongst the fences, and kicking up m-o-r-e dust, and raising m-o-r-e racket with her coughing and sneezing and blowing her nose—and always fetch up at the stand just about a neck ahead, as near as you could cipher it down.

And he had a little small bull pup, that to look at him you'd think he wa'n't worth a cent, but to set around and look ornery, and lay for a chance to steal something. But as soon as money was up on him, he was a different dog; his under-jaw'd begin to stick out like the fo'castle of a steamboat, and his teeth would uncover, and shine savage like the furnaces. And a dog might tackle him, and bully-rag him, and bite him, and throw him over his shoulder two or three times, and Andrew Jackson—which was the name of the pup—Andrew Jackson would never let on but what *he* was satisfied and hadn't expected nothing else—and the bets being doubled and doubled on the other side all the time, till the money was all up; and then all of a sudden he would grab that other dog jest by the j'int of his hind leg and freeze to it—not chaw, you understand, but only jest grip and hang on till they throwed up the sponge, if it was a year. Smiley always come out winner on that pup, till he harnessed a dog once that didn't have no hind legs, because they'd been sawed off by a circular saw, and when the thing had gone along far enough, and the money was all up, and he come to make a snatch for his pet holt, he saw in a minute how he'd been imposed on, and how the other dog had him in the door, so to speak, and he 'peared surprised, and then he looked sorter discouraged-like, and didn't try no more to win the fight, and so he got shucked out bad. He gave Smiley a look, as much as to say his heart was broke, and it was *his* fault, for putting up a dog that hadn't no hind legs for him to take holt of, which was his main dependence in a fight, and then he limped off a piece and laid down and died. It was a good pup, was that Andrew Jackson, and would have made a name for hisself if he'd lived, for the stuff was in him, and he had genius—I know it, because he hadn't had no opportunities to speak of, and it don't stand to reason that a dog could make such a fight as he could under them circumstances, if he hadn't no talent. It always makes me feel sorry when I think of that last fight of his'n, and the way it turned out.

Well, thish-yer Smiley had rat-tarriers, and chicken cocks, and tom-cats, and all them kind of things, till you couldn't rest, and you couldn't fetch nothing for him to bet on but he'd match you. He ketched a frog one day, and took him home, and said he cal'klated to edercate him; and so he never done nothing for three months but set in his back yard and learn that frog to jump. And you bet he *did* learn him, too. He'd give him a little punch behind, and the next minute you'd see that frog whirling in the air like a doughnut—see him turn one summerset, or may be a couple, if he got a good start, and come down flat-footed and all right, like a cat. He got him up so in the matter of catching flies, and kept him in practice so constant, that he'd nail a fly every time as far as he could see him. Smiley said all a frog wanted was education, and he could do most anything—and I believe him. Why, I've seen him set Dan'l Webster down here on this floor—Dan'l Webster was the name of the frog—and sing out, "Flies, Dan'l, flies!" and quicker'n you could wink, he'd spring straight up, and snake a fly off'n the counter there, and flop down on the floor again as solid as a gob of mud, and fall to scratching the side of his head with his hind foot as indifferent as if he hadn't no idea he'd been doin' any more'n any frog might do. You never see a frog so modest and straightfor'ard as he was, for all he was so gifted. And when it come to fair and square jumping on a dead level, he could get over more ground at one straddle than any animal of his breed you ever see. Jumping on a dead level was his strong suit, you understand; and when it come to that, Smiley would ante up money on him as long as he had a red. Smiley was monstrous proud of his frog, and well he might be, for fellers that had traveled and been everywheres, all said he laid over any frog that ever *they* see.

Well Smiley kept the beast in a little lattice box, and he used to fetch him down town sometimes and lay for a bet. One day a feller—a stranger in the camp, he was—come across him with his box, and says:

"What might it be that you've got in the box?"

And Smiley says, sorter indifferent like, "It might be a

parrot, or it might be a canary, may be, but it ain't—it's only just a frog."

And the feller took it, and looked at it careful, and turned it round this way and that, and says, "H'm—so 'tis. Well, what's *he* good for?"

"Well," Smiley says, easy and careless, "he's good enough for *one* thing, I should judge—he can outjump ary frog in Calaveras county."

The feller took the box again, and took another long, particular look, and give it back to Smiley, and says, very deliberate, "Well, I don't see no p'ints about that frog that's any better'n any other frog."

"May be you don't," Smiley says. "May be you understand frogs, and may be you don't understand 'em; may be you've had experience, and may be you an't only a amature, as it were. Anyways, I've got *my* opinion, and I'll risk forty dollars he can outjump any frog in Calaveras county."

And the feller studied a minute, and then says, kinder sad like, "Well, I'm only a stranger here, and I ain't got no frog, but if I had a frog, I'd bet you."

And then Smiley says, "That's all right—that's all right—if you'll hold my box a minute, I'll go and get you a frog." And so the feller took the box, and put up his forty dollars along with Smiley's, and set down to wait.

So he set there a good while thinking and thinking to hisself, and then he got the frog out and prized his mouth open and took a teaspoon and filled him full of quail shot—filled him pretty near up to his chin—and set him on the floor. Smiley he went to the swamp and slopped around in the mud for a long time, and finally he ketched a frog, and fetched him in, and give him to this feller and says:

"Now, if you're ready, set him alongside of Dan'l, with his fore-paws just even with Dan'l, and I'll give the word." Then he says, "One—two—three—jump!" and him and the feller touched up the frogs from behind, and the new frog hopped off, but Dan'l give a heave, and hysted up his shoulders—so—like a Frenchman, but it wan't no use—he couldn't budge; he was planted as solid as an anvil, and he couldn't no more stir than if he was anchored out. Smiley was a good deal surprised, and he was disgusted too, but he didn't have no idea what the matter was, of course.

The feller took the money and started away; and when he was going out at the door, he sorter jerked his thumb over his shoulders—this way—at Dan'l, and says again, very deliberate, "Well, *I* don't see no p'ints about that frog that's any better'n any other frog."

Smiley he stood scratching his head and looking down at Dan'l a long time, and at last he says, "I do wonder what in the nation that frog throw'd off for—I wonder if there ain't something the matter with him—he 'pears to look mighty baggy, somehow." And he ketched Dan'l by the nap of his neck, and lifted him up and says, "Why, blame my cats, if he don't weigh five pound!" and turned him upside down, and he belched out a double handful of shot. And then he see how it was, and he was the maddest man—he set the frog down and took out after that feller, but he never ketched him. And—

[Here Simon Wheeler heard his name called from the front yard, and got up to see what was wanted.] And turning to me as he moved away, he said: "Just set where you are, stranger, and rest easy—I an't going to be gone a second."

But, by your leave, I did not think that a continuation of the history of the enterprising vagabond *Jim* Smiley would be likely to afford me much information concerning the *Rev. Leonidas W.* Smiley, and so I started away.

At the door I met the sociable Wheeler returning, and he buttonholed me and recommenced:

"Well, thish-yer Smiley had a yaller one-eyed cow that

didn't have no tail, only jest a short stump like a bannanner, and—"

"Oh! hang Smiley and his afflicted cow!" I muttered, good-naturedly, and bidding the old gentleman good-day, I departed.

GRANT'S TAME TROUT
by Samuel T. Farquhar

This tale is probably the best-known "fish story" in American folklore. Like "The Celebrated Jumping Frog of Calaveras County," its effectiveness depends on how it is told, rather than on its intrinsic merits.

The sage of Beaver Camp sat sunning himself on the bench beside the cook camp, the bench so widely known as the scene of countless weary hours of that perpetual toiler. He seemed to be smoking an old black pipe, whereas he was only dropping matches into its empty bowl at intervals of three minutes, agreeable to the terms of his contract with the American Match trust.

As he so sat and pondered, the writer, at the time a recent arrival, approached and said: "Mr. Grant, I wish you would give me the true history of your wonderful success in taming a trout. I have heard of it in all parts of the world but I have always longed to hear the story direct from headquarters."

"Well, it really ain't so much of a story," replied the famous chronicler. "It was this way. Nine year ago the eleventh day of last June, I was fishin' out there in the pads, and right under that third yaller leaf to the right of the channel—yes, that one with the rip in it—I ketched a trout 'bout six inches long. I never see a more intelligent lookin' little feller—high

forehead, smooth face, round, dimpled chin, and a most uncommon bright, sparkling, knowin' eye.

"I always allowed that with patience and cunning a real
young trout (when they gets to a heft of 10 or 15 pounds
there ain't no teachin' them nothin') could be tamed jest like
a dog or cat.

"There was a little water in the boat and he swims around
in it all right till I goes ashore and then I gets a tub we had,
made of the half of a pork barrel, fills it with water and bores
a little small hole through the side close down to the bottom
and stops the hole with a peg.

"I sets this tub away back in a dark corner of the camp
and every night after the little fellow gets asleep I slip in, in
my stockin' feet, and pulls out the peg softly and lets out jest
a little mite of the water. I does this night after night so mighty
sly that the little chap never suspected nothin' and he was a-
livin' hale and hearty for three weeks on the bottom of that
tub as dry as a cook stove, and then I knowed he was fit for
trainin'.

"So I took him out o' doors and let him wiggle awhile on
the path and soon got to feedin' him out of my hand. Pretty
soon after that when I walked somewhat slow (I'm naturally
quite a slow walker some folks think) he could follow me right
good all round the clearin', but sometimes his fins did get ketched up in the brush jest a mite and I had to go back and swamp
out a little trail for him; bein' a trout, of course he could easy
follow a spotted line.

"Well, as time went on, he got to follerin' me most every-
where and hardly ever lost sight of me, and me and him was
great friends, sure enough.

"Near about sundown one evening, I went out to the
spring back of the camp, same one as you cross goin' to Little
Island, to get some butter out of a pail, and, of course, he
comes trottin' along behind. There was no wind that night, I

remember, and I could hear his poor little fins a-raspin' on the chips where we'd been gettin' out splits in the cedar swamp. Well, sir, he follered me close up and came out onto the logs across the brook and jest as I was a-stoopin' down over the pail I heard a kee-plunk! behind me and Gorry! If he hadn't slipped through a chink between them logs and was drowned before my very eyes before I could reach him, so he was." Here a tear started from the good old man's eye on a very dusty trip down his time-stained cheek.

"Of course I was terrible cut up at first—I couldn't do a stroke of work for three weeks—but I got to thinkin' that as it was comin' on cold (it was in late November then) and snow would soon be here and he, poor little cuss, wasn't rugged enough for snow-shoein' and he couldn't foller me afoot all winter no how, and as he couldn't live without me, mebby it was jest as well after all he was took off that way. Do you know, Mister, some folks around here don't believe a word of this, but if you'll come down to the spring with me, right now, I'll show you the very identical chink he dropped through that night, so I will. I've never allowed anyone to move it. No, sir! nor I never will."

Here the old man dropped match number thirty-seven into his pipe and sucked at it hard in silence, while I crept softly away on tiptoes. I never could bring myself to speak of it again, after seeing him so deeply moved—I never could.

THE CATS THAT CLAWED TO HEAVEN
by Percy MacKaye

This wildly exaggerated fantasy has been credited to a legendary Kentucky storyteller named Solomon Shell. The impact of the story is heightened by the narrator's picturesque diction.

Come here'n, Hanky and Henny! Quit your scratch-fightin'! Ef you leetle twin fellers starts a clawin'-match, you maht end up like the twin painter-cats done.

Where-all did *they* end? They ended plumb up in heaven, that's whar! My Gub! Air ye aimin' to haul me into court for testimony? You'll shore raise to be jedge and sheriff yit!

Well, yere's the evidence, then.——

Yis, painters is kindly overgrowed wildcats. Some calls 'em mount'in-lions. Gittin' sca'cer nowadays, but I's shot a sight in my time.

Me and Chunk Farley used to paar off and go trackin' 'em. Chunk hisself was a crack shot and 'lowed he could outaim me shootin'. But I disputed him his record. Anyways, one evenin' us come to a showdown.

Preachin' Charlie Boggs had aimed to jine us huntin' that time, but me and Chunk skun off in the middle of his sarmon. Us had ben huntin' all daylight, and no luck yit. The corn-shuckin' moon were jist uppin' her over the ridge, but she hadn't tipped to us in the shadder bottom. We was fordin' a branch. Both to onct, us stopped still, shin-deep in the tide.

Right thar on the crick bank laid a painter big's a cow-heifer. Two leetle cub-kittens was cuddlin' betwixt her paws. Tongue-lickin' em, she was, and never seen us.

Click! went our triggers to onct.

She lipt to her laigs, nosin' us, a-swarpin' her gret tail.

Bang! she rolled in the tide!

"*I* fotched her!" hollered Chunk.

"*Me,* you mean!" says I.

We had her up the bank in two jiffies, daid as a dollar.

"Right purty a hide for my ole woman," I says.

"The cat's mine," says Chunk. "Th'aint but one bullet-hole in her."

"So there ain't," says I, "but I reckon we don't start no feud, Chunk. Let's we divvy the kittens."

Well, so we done hit. Yan two leetle yaller kits was curled up thar on the moss-bank, as like as two buttons, and purty as twin peas in a pod. Chunk picks up one cub-kit, and me t'other; but yit we stands starin' at the ole daid painter.

"Tell ye what, Chunk," says I. "We'll match for her."

"How?" he axes.

"With these-yere kittens. We'll keep 'em a six-month. You raise yourn, leetle Catcher, thar; and I'll raise mine, here, leetle Scratcher. Come next spring, we'll match 'em in a fightin'-bout: and whichever feller's cat licks t'other's, the owner of the champeen wins the ole painter's hide. Meanwhiles we'll salt the hide."

"Done!" says Chunk. So us skun the painter and went home.

Soon as hit was salted, us handed hit over to Preachin' Charlie to trustee hit as ompire.

Lorsy, the rinktums I had raisin' that cub-kitten, Scratcher!

Mice and rats—he'd set up midnights on the bed-quilt and eat 'em in alive! In three days there warn't a varmint on the place left. My ole woman got moughty peeved 'cause I had to restock our rat-famine with groundhogs to keep my tom-kit fed up for the prize match. My ole sow, Chinkapin, suspicioned him and sulked she wouldn't raise no shoat-babies that fall to feed cat-flesh. So she packed off. I's tell ye later whar I found her.

Meanwhiles little kit Scratcher was biggin' and biggin' to a half-grown'd painter-cat.

Well, at last come round the six-month mornin, and here come Chunk Farley leadin' Catcher, his twin half-grown'der, in a toggle-chain. Along with him was Preachin' Charlie, totin' the ole painter's hide. Redbuds was purty abloom, and us met up to my ole smoke-house, me with my Scratcher on a hitch-rope.

Jericho! Those cats shied like they was furreigners 'stid

o' twin brothers. Bubbled up their backs like milk bilin', and spit fire and steam.

"Hold your fightin' partners!" hollers Preachin' Charlie. "Ef be I'm ompirin' this-yere cat-bout, hit's goin' to be fit out with eethical and matheematical keerectitude. First-offly we settles the handicap."

Well, sirs, us up and weighted those cats on the balancers: tipped jist even, they did; not the ace of an ounce betwixt 'em.

Nextly we measured 'em up, down, through, and acrosst, top to toe: not the haar of an inch between Catcher and Scratcher! Twins they was to a dot.

"Pint-blank even! Thar won't be no handicap," says Charlie; and then he laid down the law on our proceedin's.

Up he clumb on the smoke-house, lays hisself along the ridge-comb, retchin' out his hand with a hunk o' raw meat, which he steadies hit plump halfly on the tipnotch of the beam-saddle.

Meanwhiles, at the right-hand eaves-drip, Chunk raises his cat on the roof-slide, nose-up towards the meat, and holds on by the tail, keepin' the rump prezactly even with the eaves' aidge.

Likewisely, on the left hand, I doos the very selfsame with *my* cat.

"Right smart aimed, Fellers," says Preachin' Charlie, lookin' down, each side, moughty judeecious. "The twin nozzles is p'inted plumb straight at the target. Now, then, arter I says grace on this-yer meat, when you hears me holler, 'Haids on!' you let go tails."

So us shet our eyes whiles the preacher spoke him a few graceful words, beseechin' a heavenly guidance fer the twins. Then we hears him holler out, "Haids on!"

Bing flew the tails, and me and Chunk was seein' day-stars on our backs.

"Catcher!" Chunk yells.

"Scratcher!" I hollers.

Next thing we see was them cat-cubs top o' the ridge-comb, haids on, with their jaws lock-jammed in the middle o' that raw meat, clawin' fer heaven.

"Topple him down, Catcher! Tumble him, Scratcher!" We scritched all dad-blazes!

But hit were jist vanity of vanities, callin' 'em back. Them twins was balanced plumb even and bound for paradise.

For, ye see, Catcher was prezactly the same twin-strong-ness as Scratcher; and Scratcher was excisely the same twin-cleverness as Catcher. Neither one could outeven t'other. *Both* was champeens.

Nary cat couldn't down his twin, so the only way they could travel was *up*. And the more they nacherly clawed, the more they jist nacherly riz.

So thar they went clapper-clawin' in a yaller cloud, scratch-fightin' to glory, fur flyin' like goose feathers, on up, neck and neck, nail and toe, crop and crupper, away on, spout-up'ards, like a razzle o' dead leaves in a whirl-storm.

Last thing us seen was a little fog-skiff, fadin' out, like the old moon by daytime, the fur feathers snowin' down.

"Dad-fetch ye, Preachin' Charlie!" says I. "What made ye so plumb matheematical?"

"What-all in tarnation did ye speak that heavenly grace fer?" axes Chunk, moughty sulkin'.

Preachin' Charlie slid down off the roof.

"I reckon, fellers," says he, "you won't be needin' me for ompire agin till the next jedgment risin'. Meanwhiles I'll jist trustee this-here salted hide."

So he went on home, packin' the ole painter's skin with him.

Poor Chunk he never come back to that smoke-house till six months arter then. Hit were corn-shuckin' time, our huntin' day come round agin.

I met him thar, and we stood neck and neck, starin' uply.—

The fur was fallin' thar yit.

SUNRISE IN HIS POCKET
by Davy Crockett

Davy Crockett, whose real life was almost as fantastic as the legendary tales about him, may or may not have written the following tall story. At any rate, it presents a good example of the "larger-than-life" frontier demigod.

One January morning it was so all-screwen-up cold that the forest trees war so stiff that they couldn't shake, and the very day-break froze fast as it war tryin' to dawn. The tinder-box in my cabin would no more ketch fire than a sunk raft at the bottom o' the sea. Seein' that daylight war so far behind time, I thought creation war in a fair way for freezin' fast.

"So," thinks I, "I must strike a leetle fire from my fingers, light my pipe, travel out a few leagues, and see about it."

Then I brought my knuckles together like two thunder clouds, but the sparks froze up afore I could begin to collect 'em—so out I walked, and endeavored to keep myself unfriz by goin' at a hop, step and jump gait, and whistlin' the tune of "fire in the mountains!" as I went along in three double quick time. Well, arter I had walked about twenty-five miles up the peak o' Daybreak Hill, I soon discovered what war the matter. The airth had actually friz fast in her axis, and couldn't turn round; the sun had got jammed between two cakes o' ice under the wheels, an' thar he had bin shinin' and workin' to get loose, till he friz fast in his cold sweat.

"C-r-e-a-t-i-o-n!" thought I, "this are the toughest sort o' suspension, and it mustn't be endured—somethin' must be done, or human creation is done for."

It war then so antedeluvian and premature cold that my upper and lower teeth an' tongue war all collapsed together as tight as a friz oyster. I took a fresh twenty pound bear off o' my back that I'd picked up on the road, an' beat the animal agin the ice till the hot ile began to walk out on him at all sides. I then took an' held him over the airth's axes, an' squeezed him till I thaw'd 'em loose, poured about a ton on it over the sun's face, give the airth's cog-wheel one kick backward, till I got the sun loose—whistled "Push along, keep movin'!" an' in about fifteen seconds the airth gin a grunt, and begun movin'—the sun walked up beautiful, salutin' me with sich a wind o' gratitude that it made me sneeze. I lit my pipe by the blaze o' his top-knot, shouldered my bear, an' walked home, introducin' the people to fresh daylight with a piece of sunrise in my pocket, with which I cooked my bear steaks, an' enjoyed one o' the best breakfasts I had tasted for some time. If I didn't, jist wake some mornin' and go with me to the office o' sunrise!

NECKTIE JUSTICE

by Ruel McDaniel

Judge Roy Bean, the self-styled "Law West of the Pecos," was only one of a number of Western jurists whose exploits have become part of American folklore. This account of his adventures is probably not historically accurate, but it does reveal the personality and character of Judge Bean. His flowery address to the condemned prisoner has also been attributed to other Western judges, including Judge Parker (the "Hanging Judge") of Fort Smith.

"Hear ye! Hear ye! This honorable court's now in session; and if any galoot wants a snort afore we start, let him step up to the bar and name his pizen. Oscar, serve the gentlemen." Thus did Judge Bean open court to try one Carlos Robles, an opening typical of his original procedure.

"Carlos Robles," he said solemnly after witnesses and

hangers-on had downed their liquor, "it is the findin' of this court that you are charged with a grave offense against the peace and dignity of the law West of the Pecos and the State of Texas, to wit; cattle-rustlin'. Guilty or not guilty?"

Not being able to speak or comprehend English, Robles merely grunted. "Court accepts yore plea of guilt. The jury will now deliberate; and if it brings a verdict short of hangin' it'll be declared in contempt. Gentlemen, is your verdict ready?"

The twelve nondescript citizens cleared their throats in unison. "It is, your honor," several spoke.

"Thank you, gentlemen. Stand up, Carlos Robles, and receive yore sentence. You got anything to say why judgment shouldn't be passed on you in this court?"

Of course Carlos had not, in view of the fact that he had only the vaguest idea of what was transpiring.

"Carlos Robles," Judge Roy continued, his voice almost quaking with the solemnity of the occasion, "you been tried by twelve true and good men, not men of yore peers, but as high above you as heaven is of hell; and they've said you're guilty of rustlin' cattle.

"Time will pass and seasons will come and go; Spring with its wavin' green grass and heaps of sweet-smellin' flowers on every hill and in every dale. Then will come sultry Summer, with her shimmerin' heat-waves on the baked horizon; and Fall, with her yeller harvest-moon and the hills growin' brown and golden under a sinkin' sun; and finally Winter, with its bitin', whinin' wind, and all the land will be mantled with snow. But you won't be here to see any of 'em, Carlos Robles; not by a dam' sight, because it's the order of this court that you be took to the nearest tree and hanged by the neck till you're dead, dead, dead, you olive-colored son-of-a-billy-goat!"

The Law West of the Pecos could be cruel in administering his brand of justice; but he was cruel only when he deemed the accused and the crime fully warranting such cruelty. He more frequently tempered justice with his own peculiar brand of mercy, especially if there was any means by which he could profit by that mercy.

One afternoon several ranchmen brought in a twenty-year old boy accused of horse-stealing. They demanded that he be tried and dealt with according to the enormity of the crime.

Judge Bean duly opened court. He appointed six men as jurors, the actual number meaning nothing to him and depending entirely upon men available. He would not appoint just any citizens to jury duty. They must be good customers of the liquor bar at the other end of the shack during intermissions, or their services as jurors no longer were desirable or acceptable. Every transaction must be made to return the utmost in profit, and non-drinking jurors were strictly dead timber.

"Hear ye! This honorable court is again in session. Anyone wishin' a snort, have it now. This here prisoner is charged with the grave offense of stealin' a horse and Oscar, where are the witnesses?" the Law West of the Pecos opened. He appreciated his own sense of humor in varying his court openings to relieve the monotony; but he seldom varied to the extent of omitting the invitation to participate in a snort at the other bar.

"We caught him in the act of stealin' the animal," the ranchman testified. "He admitted his intentions."

"That right, young feller? You was stealin' the cayuse?"

The young prisoner dropped his head, unruly red hair tumbling down over his high forehead. "Yes, Your Honor," he mumbled.

"Gentlemen of the jury," His Honor instructed, "the accused pleads guilty to horse theft. You know as well as I do the penalty. I'm ready for yore verdict." And it was promptly forthcoming.

Gravely the judge passed sentence. "If there's any last word, or anything, I'll give you a few minutes," he told the pale Easterner, thus extending an infrequent favor.

"I would like to write a note—to my mother back in Pennsylvania," the doomed prisoner mumbled with obvious emotion. "Thank you."

"Oscar, fetch the prisoner a piece of wrappin' paper and a pencil. I think we got a pencil back there behind that row of bottles." Bean gently handed the convicted thief these writing facilities, got up and tendered him the beer barrel and rickety table from which sentence had just been passed. Then he took a position directly behind the boy so that he could watch over his shoulder at what he wrote.

The victim wrote at length in apology for the grief and trouble he had caused his mother and earnestly sought her forgiveness. "In small part perhaps I can repay you for the money I have cost you in keeping me out of trouble. Enclosed is $400, which I've saved. I want you—."

Judge Bean started, cleared his throat, cut in at this point. "By gobs!" he exclaimed, "gentlemen, I got a feelin' there's been a miscarriage of justice, in this case. I hereby declare it re-opened. Face the bar, young man."

The prisoner removed himself from the beer keg and stood erect in front of the judicial bench, befuddled at this sudden turn.

"After all, that wasn't much of a cayuse the lad tried to steal; and he didn't actually steal him. So I rule it's a finable case. I hereby fine the accused three hundred dollars and get to hell outer this country afore I change my mind!"

The boy gladly enough paid three hundred of his four hundred dollars and assured the court that the next setting sun would find his brow well beyond El Rio Pecos.

Practically every cattleman and law-abiding citizen of the Bean bailiwick had an indefinite appointment as deputy constable to the Law West of the Pecos. Thus any citizen who apprehended any person in the act of committing a crime or suspected any of crime had authority to bring him on forthwith for trial. Bean consistently encouraged such co-operation, for the more business they brought before the court, the greater the financial returns for the whole establishment. Naturally it was understood that such arresting constables did not in any manner participate in the fee accruing from such cases created by them. This doubtless was the only justice court in the State of Texas wherein only one official received all fees collected by the office.

Under authority as deputy constable, Reb Wise, Pecos rancher, brought in a cattle rustler on a hot August afternoon when business at the refreshment counter was exceptionally brisk. It was all both Roy and Oscar could do to handle the trade. Consequently Bean looked up with sour expression when Deputy Constable Wise approached the bar and informed the judge that a prisoner was awaiting attention at the bar of justice.

"What's he charged with, Reb?" Roy asked, opening another foaming bottle of Triple-X beer.

"Cattle-rustlin', yuhr honor," Reb replied.

"Whose cattle?"

"Mine."

"You positive he's guilty, Reb?"

"Positive? Say, Judge, I caught him with a runnin' iron on one of my finest calves!" the rancher replied with emphasis.

For the first time Roy glanced up at the scowling prisoner. He noticed blood dripping from his left ear. "Who plugged his ear?" he inquired.

"I did, yuhr honor, when he wouldn't stop."

"You ought'n shot at his head, Reb. You could 'a' killed him; and that would 'a' been bad, because he wouldn't have been saved for the punishment he deserves. You real shore he's guilty?"

"Didn't I say, Judge, I caught him runnin' a brand on my stuff?"

"All right then," the judge said. "What'll it be for you, feller?" to a newcomer at the bar, ". . . All right then. The court finds the accused guilty as charged; and as there ain't no worse punishment I know of right handy, I hereby sentence him to be hung. Reb, I'm busy's hell here. You and some of yore compadres take him out and tie his neck to some handy limb—some place where his cronies'll be positive to see him; and that's my rulin'. Court's adjourned and what'll it be for you down there, Slim?"

III. Tales of the Frontier

TALKING IT OVER

1. a) How was the narrator in "The Celebrated Jumping Frog of Calaveras County" tricked into hearing the story? Why do you think his friend did it?
   b) How did Mark Twain improve on the original printed version of the "Jumping Frog" story?

2. In "Grant's Tame Trout," how does "the sage of Beaver Camp" offer to "prove" the truth of his tale? What is his listener's attitude throughout the story? Is it sincere?

3. The tale-spinners in "The Celebrated Jumping Frog of Calaveras County" and "Grant's Tame Trout" both appeared to be naïve country bumpkins, but their technique of telling a tall tale effectively required real artistry. Analyze their techniques. What effect were they striving for? How could a less experienced raconteur have spoiled the stories? For more information on this topic, read "How to Tell a Story," by Mark Twain.

4. What are the characteristics of tall tales, using the first five stories in this chapter as typical examples?

5. In "Necktie Justice," what is your opinion of Judge Bean's brand of "justice"? Why did the people of Texas tolerate judges like Bean? Why did Roy Bean become a legend?

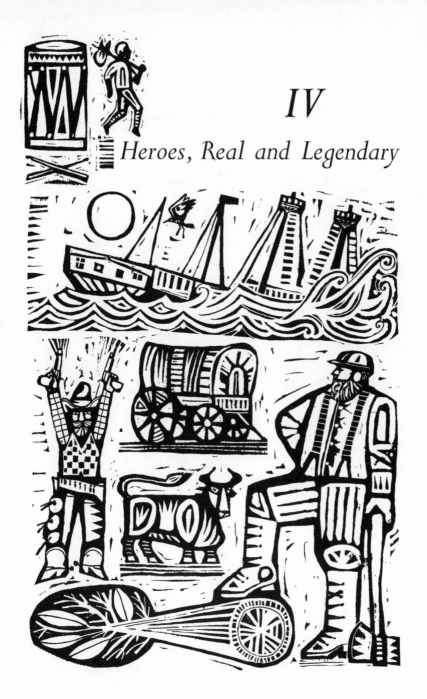

IV
Heroes, Real and Legendary

From earliest recorded times to the present, mankind has needed heroes. Although the word "hero" has come to mean many things, let us consider it to mean an individual who, through his actions and character, personifies the most honored values of his people. For example, Theseus, the legendary hero of ancient Greece, was admired by Athenians not only for his strength and courage, but also for his clever mind and leadership abilities, two traits held in high esteem in Athens. The rest of Greece, however, placed primary emphasis on physical prowess, which explains why their hero was Hercules, a man who was strong enough and brave enough to challenge the gods, but who was also impulsive, destructive, intellectually limited, and incapable of leadership.

Early America, lacking a unified set of values, had many heroes, representing numerous occupational, ethnic, and regional groups. Some of these heroes, like Davy Crockett and Jim Bowie, were real men whose exploits inflamed the imagination of poets and storytellers, until today it is often hard to tell where the facts end and the folklore begins. Others, like Paul Bunyan and Pecos Bill, obviously never existed in the historical sense. They came into being, and flourished, because they represented Young America: independent, hardworking, inventive and, above all, supremely confident. In this chapter, the reader will meet a few of the many characters, real and legendary, who make up the heroic tradition in America.

THE WAVING OF THE SPECTRAL ARMS
by Archibald Rutledge

Mobile Jones was an authentic folk hero of the Carolinas. In this story, he proves that a cool head is just as important as physical strength, when one is faced by a superhuman monster.

The wreck of a great sailing ship is strangely haunting and luring, especially if that wreck has lain for years in the wild surf of a lonely beach. On the strand of Murphy's Island near the mouths of the Santee River in South Carolina, the hulk of *The Western Wave* had lain for fifteen years. A four-master in the coastal lumber trade, she had been beached in the gale of September 1893 and had been abandoned as a total loss. Just within the line of white horses she lay, a hundred yards from shore at high tide. Sunk in the treacherous sands and listed heavily to starboard, on the full tide she was swept from stem to stern by the bull-mouthed breakers. At low water it was possible to walk out to the wreck, to climb aboard and to walk her deserted deck, but neither as a business nor as a pastime was this practice especially attractive. In fact, only Mobile ever went there regularly. He had found that the very best sheepshead fishing along that part of the coast was to be had at the grave of the once stately vessel.

When his trapping season was over and the fishing season had begun, in his little dugout cypress canoe Mobile would paddle down the river to the island, walk through the semi-tropical woods to the beach, wade out to the wreck, climb aboard the hulk and in the course of three hours' fishing would land from fifteen to twenty sheepshead from three to six pounds in weight. And it was all in his day's work for him to paddle the seven miles home and then walk nine miles through the pinelands to the seacoast village where his catch could be sold. If luck had been good, he would do the same thing again the next day.

Mobile nearly always hunted and fished alone. One summer, however, word of his prowess with the sheepshead reached the ears of West McConnor, a mulatto living up the river from Mobile. West was small, wiry and supple and had persistence and cunning. It was not long before West had arranged to go with the black giant to fish from the wreck of *The Western Wave.*

Perhaps no shores in the world have the same melancholy beauty, the same mournful loveliness, the same rich aspect of autumn as have the banks of the Santee in its lower reaches. The momentous pines tower in dewy sleep, the giant moss-draped cypresses stand like ancient priestesses in attitudes of prayer and the lonely reedlands stretch away from the mysterious river to the more mysterious delta. And night and day there is the pounding of the surf, declaring the might of the ocean.

Mobile felt few of these influences as he made his lithe canoe speed down the river. West felt them however, partly because he was not accustomed to them and partly because he was by disposition easily frightened.

Mobile wanted him to sit quietly in the canoe, but West wanted to turn his head and talk. "Mobile," he said, "how long you been comin' down here?"

"Ever since hatchet was a hammer," Mobile chuckled.

"You ain't never had no trouble?" West inquired, awed now by the spaciousness of marshland and river mouth and by the incessant thunder of the surf.

"Not so much," Mobile replied, remembering the time that he had tried conclusions with the sixteen-foot bull alligator that had disputed his entrance to Atkinson's Creek, and the time when in smoking a rabbit out of a hollow he had smoked out a huge diamondback rattlesnake instead.

West shivered a little. Not so much coming from a man

as conservative as Mobile did not sound very reassuring. The mulatto sat silent for a while. Then, clearing his throat, he asked with assumed indifference, "You ain't never seen no hant down here, is you?"

"Not so many," Mobile replied cheerfully, thinking of the time when, standing on the beach and looking out toward the wreck of *The Western Wave,* he had seen what appeared to be spectral arms waving above the deck. Nine seamen had been drowned when the vessel had gone to her doom. Were these the ghosts of those men? Or were phantom hands trying to raise the phantom sails? Mobile did not know, and he thought it wise not to let West in on these unsubstantial details.

"What do you mean, not so many?" asked West.

"Don't be scared," the other replied with a large assurance. "We goin' to get home all right."

"I ain't much for hants. You remember that, Mobile," West warned.

"Nobody ain't much for them," Mobile agreed, "but don't let that worry you."

"Another thing I don't understand," West persisted. "Why you always carry that big knife in your belt, Mobile?"

"To clean fish," Mobile answered. "And for other things too," he added enigmatically.

When Mobile and West landed on the placid back beach of Murphy's Island, all was sunshine, flowers, bird song. The loveliness of the place put down all thought of danger. Mobile had timed his trip so that he would reach the wreck on the young flood tide. From then until the half tide the fishing would be best. Without mishap they waded out to the wreck and climbed aboard. The air was cool, the sun bright, the fishing good. After West had landed a nine-pound sheepshead, all thought of hants completely left his mind.

West was standing by the battered and rusted capstan in the bow. The waves were rushing in fast, sweeping along the scuppers of the tilted vessel, vehemently foaming and hur-

rying on their ancient tireless task. Mobile had braced himself
beside the rail in the stern, and he had been busy hauling in
the ponderous stocky sheepsheads that for some time he had
not even turned toward his companion.

Now a sudden wild cry from West made Mobile drop
his line and instinctively start from his post toward the bow
of the wreck. "Mobile! Mobile!" yelled his friend frantically.
"Quick, Mobile!"

The footing was so treacherous on the sloping slippery
deck that Mobile, holding the rail now awash with the tide,
had to force himself through the surging water. Mobile saw
West writhing as if in agony. Was he suddenly stricken with
something? Could he have been crushed in the old mechan-
ism of the winch beside the capstan? Mobile could not tell as
he plunged warily forward toward his comrade. The warm
green waves slithered along the deck, the sunshine was wide
and bright, the woods on the island glimmered in serenity, but
here was a tragedy, grim and instant. Mobile came to a sway-
ing halt, looking forward and up to the capstan. West's cries
continued but now they sounded smothered.

Over the rail ten feet beyond him Mobile saw three huge
fleshy arms. They extended up toward the capstan. Two of
them were around West, one about his neck. They were as
taut as bowstrings, drawing, drawing down. West was fighting for his life, but the great octopus had him fast. A big string
of sheepsheads which West had tied near the rail had attracted
him out of his lair in the hold of the wreck, where a huge
breach in the ship's side gave him access. The monster with
his ten-foot arms, lined along their underside with their dreadful suckers, had firm hold on his prey. West had been so busy
with his fishing that he had not seen the tentacles slithering
over the wet rail, and one of them had him before he knew
of his danger.

Close to the side of the vessel now appeared the vast
bulk of the creature: the staring eyes, the cruel mouth with

its beak like that of a monstrous parrot. And there were other arms, some anchoring the sinister demon to the sides of the aperture in the flank of the wreck, some moving gropingly on the surface of the water, some coming over the rail.

In his life in the lonely woods and on the waters of that solitary coast Mobile had had many adventures, but the creatures he had encountered before had been well-known to him —white sharks, grim bull alligators, huge diamondback rattlers. Nothing he had ever seen could compare with this fiendish thing. No more than a few seconds could have passed from the time that Mobile paused to take in the situation until he advanced to the attack. Three tentacles had West in their grasp. He was almost fainting from exhaustion and fear. Dimly he could see Mobile below him, coming to his rescue, but he had little hope that Mobile, for all his bravery and physical power, could save him from a monstrous demon like this.

Holding the wet rail with his left hand and trying to get a firm stance on the edge of the submerged deck, Mobile drew his heavy hunting knife and slashed savagely at the first of the long tentacles. Tough as a huge rubber cable, the arm seemed to resist strength and steel. But the Negro hacked furiously, edging closer, now dodging another tentacle waving its heavy bulk above his head. In a few moments the persistence of Mobile's attack began to tell. The tentacle released its hold of West, and its horrible length dropped to the deck as Mobile severed it at the rail.

Valiantly the Negro attacked the second leathery arm, but at his first stroke he went a little off balance. The long blade of his knife tore through the arm of the octopus and struck the top of the steel rail a glancing blow. Mobile's only weapon was literally driven out of his hand. It flashed in the sunlight and then was gone beneath the boiling waters. Defenseless and with no means of attack, Mobile faced the octopus which, at the loss of one tentacle, had risen to the surface.

Gripping the rail with both hands, Mobile looked back

at West, who was still clinging desperately to the capstan. On the incline of that slippery deck he could not hope to tear the tentacles loose from him. As long as the man could keep his hold he was not doomed, but if he lost it one of those powerful arms would lift him bodily and plunge him into the sea.

Nowhere on the deck could Mobile see anything which might be turned into a weapon. The vessel had been partly salvaged and little had been left save the hulk itself. Mobile had only his bare hands and the superb strength of his glistening body. He had a plan, also, a desperate one. His friend's life was at stake, and it was Mobile who had brought him to this fatal place.

Over the rail he climbed, his great muscles bulging. He let himself warily down into the dredging tide that was wildly ramping past the wreck. Down he went until his feet touched the hard sands of the bottom, the waters swirling about his neck. He was now under the arms of the monster and within reach of his Calibanlike body. He opened the blade of his pocketknife, utterly unsuited for such an emergency, and buried it, time after time, in the body of the hideous chimera. Battered and bruised and thrust violently about, Mobile still held on. He saw the waters all about him dyed purple. The monster's struggles became more feeble. Under his own strength Mobile could feel a vaster strength ebbing away. He looked upward and saw that West was free. He was huddled exhausted over the capstan but he was out of the enemy's grasp. Then Mobile caught the upper rail and swung himself to the deck.

An hour later Mobile and West had reached home. That very night West walked all the way to the seacoast village where he sold his sheepshead for three dollars. This entire amount he invested in a heavy-bladed hunting knife, which he presented to Mobile, saying with an air of mock resentment, "Don't you use me for bait the next time you want to kill your hants."

Davy Crockett Stories

Davy Crockett's real life, culminating in his death at the Alamo, was almost as intriguing as the many tales celebrating his legendary exploits. During the 1830's, tall tales by and about Crockett achieved wide popularity and helped create a stereotyped image of the American frontiersman. These two short tales are good examples of this genre.

A RIPROARIOUS FIGHT ON THE MISSISSIPPI RIVER

by Davy Crockett

One day as I was sitting in the stern of my broad horn, the old Free and Easy, on the Mississippi, taking a horn of midshipman's grog, with a tin pot in each hand, first a draught of whiskey, and then one of river water, who should float down past me but Joe Snag; he was in a snooze, as fast as a church, with his mouth wide open; he had been ramsquaddled with whiskey for a fortnight, and as it evaporated from his body it looked like the steam from a vent pipe. Knowing the feller would be darned hard to wake, with all this steam on, as he floated past me I hit him a crack over his knob with my big steering oar. He waked in a thundering rage. Says he, halloe stranger, who axed you to crack my lice? Says I, shut up your mouth, or your teeth will get sunburnt. Upon this he crooked up his neck and neighed like a stallion. I clapped my arms and crowed like a cock. Says he, if you are a game chicken

I'll pick all the pin feathers off of you. For some time back I had been so wolfy about the head and shoulders that I was obliged to keep kivered up in a salt crib to keep from spiling, for I had not had a fight for as much as ten days. Says I, give us none of your chin music, but set your kickers on land, and I'll give you a severe licking. The fellow now jumped ashore, and he was so tall he could not tell when his feet were cold. He jumped up a rod. Says he, take care how I lite on you, and he gave a real sockdologer that made my very liver and lites turn to jelly. But he found me a real scrouger. I brake three of his ribs, and he knocked out five of my teeth and one eye. He was the severest colt that ever I tried to break. I finally got a bite hold that he could not shake off. We were now parted by some boatmen, and we were so exorsted that it was more than a month before either could have a fight. It seemed to me like a little eternity. And although I didn't come out second best, I took care not to wake up a ring-taled roarer with an oar again.

A SENSIBLE VARMINT

by Davy Crockett

Almost every boddy that knows the forrest, understands parfectly well that Davy Crockett never loses powder and ball, havin' ben brort up to blieve it a sin to throw away amminition, and that is the bennefit of a vartuous eddikation. I war out in the forrest won arternoon, and had jist got to a plaice called the grate gap, when I seed a rakkoon setting all alone upon a tree. I klapped the breech of Brown Betty to my sholder, and war jist a going to put a piece of led between his sholders, when he lifted one paw, and sez he, "Is your name Crockett?"

Sez I, "You are rite for wonst, my name is Davy Crockett."

"Then," sez he, "you needn't take no further trubble, for I may as well cum down without another word"; and the cretur wauked rite down from the tree, for he considered himself shot.

I stoops down and pats him on the head, and sez I, "I hope I may be shot myself before I hurt a hare of your head, for I never had sich a kompliment in my life."

"Seeing as how you say that," sez he, "I'll jist walk off for the present, not doubting your word a bit, d'ye see, but lest you should kinder happen to change your mind."

JAMES BOWIE TO THE RESCUE

by Herbert Asbury

James Bowie, who like Davy Crockett, perished at the Alamo, was best known for his invention of the bowie knife. According to B. A. Botkin, "The fighting knight-errant of the steam-boats, Jim Bowie—rough-and-tumble scion of a distinguished Maryland family—made a chivalrous hobby of rescuing suckers from river sharpers." This story describes one such rescue.

The river sharpers often went to great trouble and expense in setting the stage of their operations, and usually their elaborate and well-planned schemes were successful. Sometimes, however, the gamblers came to grief at the last moment, either by the quarry becoming suspicious or through interference on the part of chivalrous passengers. One of the busiest of these knights-errant of the steamboats was no less a personage than the redoubtable James Bowie, inventor of the bowie-knife, once an associate of the pirate Jean Lafitte, and the most noted duelist of his time. This noble-minded killer, who died

with Davy Crockett in the defense of the Alamo in 1836, was
a menace to the river gamblers for several years; he spent
considerable time on the lower Mississippi, and seems to have
made a practice of ferreting out crooked gamblers, beating
them at their own game, and restoring to suckers the money of
which they had been fleeced. But he always required the sucker to swear a solemn oath that he would gamble no more.

Bowie's most celebrated exploit of this character was performed on the steamer *New Orleans* in the fall of 1832, when
he saved a young gentleman of Natchez from dishonor and
a suicide's grave. In the summer of that year this young gentleman, who fancied himself as a card player and a man of the
world, went to New York on his honeymoon, and while there
collected about $50,000 on behalf of various merchants and
planters of Natchez. A syndicate of gamblers was formed to
despoil him, and one of the sharpers was sent to New York,
where he made the young gentleman's acquaintance and learned that the latter intended to go home by way of Pittsburgh
and Louisville, with a stopover of several days in Louisville
to visit relatives. When the young gentleman took a boat at
Pittsburgh the sharper was on board, and so were two "Louisiana planters," who made themselves very agreeable. Twenty-
card poker was introduced, and the young man from Natchez
was permitted to win several hundred dollars. By the time the
boat reached Louisville the four men had become such friends
that the "planters" and the sharper, who posed as a New Orleans merchant, agreed to wait and go down the river on the
New Orleans, on which the young gentleman had booked passage for himself and his bride.

The gamblers went after the young gentleman in earnest
when the *New Orleans* left the wharf at Louisville. In a few
sessions they had cheated him out of $45,000, and he was
betting frantically in a desperate effort to retrieve his losses.
Bowie, wearing a black, broad-brimmed slouch hat and black

broadcloth clothing of clerical cut, boarded the boat at Vicksburg and became an interested spectator of the game, which he saw immediately was crooked. After a few more hours' play the young man's last dollar vanished into the capacious pockets of the gamblers, and crazed by remorse he rushed to the rail and attempted to throw himself into the river. He was restrained by Bowie and his wife and taken to his cabin, where Bowie instructed that he be closely watched.

Bowie then went to the bar, casually displayed a bulging wallet, and asked for change for a hundred dollar bill. One of the gamblers, who were opening wine to celebrate the success of their *coup,* obliged, and after a few moments of conversation suggested a card game, to which Bowie agreed. On the first few hands Bowie won, and then the sharpers began to forge ahead. At length one of the "planters" dealt Bowie a hand which any poker player would bet as long as he could see, and which Bowie recognized as being intended for the big cleanup. The "planters" dropped out after a few bets, but Bowie and the "merchant" continued to raise each other until $70,000 was piled on the table between them. Finally Bowie saw what he had been watching for—the gambler's hand flicking quickly into his sleeve. Like lightning Bowie seized the sharper's wrist, at the same time drawing from his shirt-bosom a wicked-looking knife.

"Show your hand!" he commanded. "If it contains more than five cards I shall kill you!"

The gambler attempted to break loose, but Bowie twisted his wrist and his cards fell to the table—four aces, a queen and a jack.

"I shall take the pot," said Bowie, "with a legitimate poker hand, four kings and a ten."

"Who the devil are you, anyway?" cried the discomfited gambler.

"I," said the famous duelist, "am James Bowie!"

"The voice was like velvet," says an account of the affair, "but it cut like steel into the hearts of the chief gambler's confederates and deterred them from any purpose or impulse they might have had to interfere. They, with the crowd, shrank back from the table, smitten with terror by the name. Bowie softly swept the banknotes into his large slouch hat and lightly clapped it on his head."

There are two versions of what happened next. One is that Bowie let the gambler go with a lecture, but kept the pot. The other is that the sharper insisted on a duel, and that Bowie borrowed a pistol and shot him off the wheelhouse "just as the great round face of the sun, like a golden cannon ball," appeared over a neighboring cliff. This trifling matter disposed of, Bowie gave the young gentleman of Natchez two-thirds of the contents of the hat, and kept the remainder as spoils of war. With tears in his eyes the young gentleman swore never to touch another card, and both he and his bride prayed that Heaven might bless their benefactor.

MIKE FINK AND THE KICKING SHERIFF

by Walter Blair and Franklin J. Meine

Davy Crockett's tall tales created the stereotyped "ring-tailed roarer" frontier character, but Mike Fink, a Mississippi River keelboatman, was the genuine article. In this story, Fink, a notorious brawler and braggart, is taught a much-needed lesson.

[A] tale apparently circulated orally for years—for it did not find its way into print until 1895—told how Mike was quieted at the hands—or rather the feet—of the sheriff of the tiny town of Westport [Indiana], opposite Louisville on the Ohio.

Mike was telling jokes one day in the grocery (grog shop), and all of the drinkers laughed heartily, uproariously, at his yarns—all save one man, a little dried up fellow whose pensive face suggested that he was contemplating death and eternity.

Mike at last walked over to him.

"See here, Mister," he said, "these yarns I been tellin' is funny, and you stand there as glum as a dead catfish on a sandbar. I tell snorters for folk to laugh at in a good humored way, an' by God, I don't let no man make light of 'em."

"Is that so?" the little man asked, negligently, and he sank back into his gloomy contemplation.

Mike, at the bar, told another yarn, and the company dutifully howled. But the little man, sternly watched by Mike, looked positively tearful. Mike stamped across the floor.

"Whoop!" yelled Mike. "Calamity's a-comin'! I'm a Salt River roarer, an' I'm chockful o' fight. I'm——"

But in the middle of his boast, Mike was surprised. For the wizened mourner suddenly leaped into the air and as his body swooped downward, his fist smacked Mike below the ear, and the keeler fell sprawling.

"Is that so?" said his opponent, and he lay down as if to rest.

Mike staggered to his feet, blood in his eye, roaring with anger. But as he came forward, the little man doubled into a tangle of flaying feet and clawing fists. Mike went into a whirl of flying arms and legs, and emerged with a scratched face and a sinking in his stomach where a swift kick had landed. Angrier than ever, he flopped on the man again; and again, against the torrent of claws and leaping boots, he was able to do nothing. Four times more he tried in vain to seize or to strike his rival, and each time, Mike looked more as if calamity and desolation had struck him.

"Stranger," panted Mike at last, "I'm free to own I can't do nothin' with you. You're tougher to chaw nor buckskin."

"Is that so?" dreamily asked the visitor. "Listen to me. I'm Ned Taylor, sheriff of this county; and if you and your crew don't get the hell out of here in ten minutes, I'll arrest the mess of ye!"

"Five's enough," said Mike, according to the tale. "You're a snag, a riffle, and a sawyer all in one."

And the people who handed down the tale maintain that the sheriff said, "Is that so?" and resumed his gloomy contemplation.

BRAS COUPÉ
by Herbert Asbury

This runaway slave, so named because one of his arms had been amputated, became a fearful symbol of Negro retribution to white slaveowners.

One of the famous Bamboula dancers of the early days, and also an expert wielder of the beef bones, was a gigantic Negro owned by General William de Buys, who is said to have been the first to attach little bells to his ankles instead of the customary bits of metal. He could leap higher and shout louder than any of the other slaves who stamped and cavorted in the dance; his stamping, indeed, shook the ground, and when he cried: "Badoum! Badoum!" the tops of the sycamore-trees trembled and swayed in the wind caused by his mighty bellowings. And in his ham-like fists the beef bones rattled upon the head of the Bamboula drum with a crashing roar that resembled nothing less than a salvo of artillery fire. His name during the period of his fame as a Bamboula artist was Squier; a few years later, as Bras Coupé and the Brigand of the Swamp, he acquired a different sort of renown.

General de Buys was well known in New Orleans as a

remarkably kind and indulgent master; he petted, coddled, and spoiled the Negro Squier, taught him to shoot, and permitted him to go alone on hunting expeditions in the forests adjacent to the city. And Squier practiced assiduously with the General's rifle; premonition, he said afterwards, warned him that he would eventually lose an arm, and so he became an expert marksman with either hand alone. The taste of freedom which Squier experienced on his journeys into the woods after game was too much for him. He began running away, and received only slight punishment when he was captured and returned to General de Buys. Early in 1834 Squier was shot by a patrol of planters searching the swamps for runaway slaves, and his right arm was amputated, whence the sobriquet Bras Coupé, by which he was thereafter known. As soon as his injury had healed, Bras Coupé fled into the swamps and organized a gang of escaped blacks and a few renegade white men, whom he led on frequent robbing and murdering forays on the outskirts of the city, with an occasional venture into the thickly settled residential districts. He was New Orleans' most feared outlaw for nearly three years, and the successor of the *Kaintock* as the hobgoblin with which nurses and mothers frightened the Creole children. Reviewing his career, the *Picayune* after his death described him as "a semi-devil and a fiend in human shape," and said that his life had been "one of crime and depravity."

Among the slaves Bras Coupé soon became a legendary figure endowed with superhuman powers; in the folklore of the New Orleans Negroes he was installed alongside the redoubtable Annie Christmas and in many respects was accounted her superior. He was, of course, fireproof and invulnerable to wounds, for he was familiar with the miraculous herbs described by the French travelers Bossu, Perrin du Lac, and Baudry des Loziéres, and with many others which these avid searchers after botanical wonders had not discovered.

Hunters returned to New Orleans from the swamps and told how, having encountered Bras Coupé, they fired at him, only to see their bullets flatten against his chest; some even said that the missiles had bounced off the iron-like body of the outlaw and whizzed dangerously close to their own heads, while Bras Coupé laughed derisively and strode grandly into the farthest reaches of the swamps. And according to the slave tradition, detachments of soldiers sent after him vanished in a cloud of mist. Moreover, his very glance paralyzed, if he so wished, and he fed on human flesh.

The popular belief in Bras Coupé's invulnerability received a rude shock when, on April 6, 1837, he was wounded by two hunters who braved his magical powers and shot him near the Bayou St. John. And it was dissipated entirely on July 19 of the same year. On that day a Spanish fisherman named Francisco Garcia, who was known to the slaves as a friend of Bras Coupé's, drove slowly through the streets of New Orleans a cart drawn by a decrepit mule, and watched with tender solicitude an ungainly bundle, wrapped in old sacks, which jounced in the bed of the vehicle. Garcia stopped in front of Cabildo and carried his bundle into the office of Mayor Dennis Prieur, where he unwrapped it and disclosed the body of Bras Coupé. The fisherman told the authorities that on the day before, the 18th, he was fishing in the Bayou St. John when Bras Coupé fired at him and missed, whereupon the indignant fisherman went ashore and beat out the brigand's brains with a club. The truth, however, appears to have been that Bras Coupé was slain as he slept in the fisherman's hut. Garcia demanded the immediate payment of the two-thousand-dollar reward which he had heard had been offered for Bras Coupé dead or alive, but he received only two hundred and fifty dollars. The body of the outlaw was exposed in the Place d'Armes for two days, and several thousand slaves were compelled to march past and look at it, as a warning.

HIGH JOHN DE CONQUER

by Zora Neale Hurston

High John de Conquer was pure legend, but he lived a very real existence in the imaginations of plantation Negroes waiting to regain their freedom and self-respect.

Maybe, now, we used-to-be-black African folks can be of some help to our brothers and sisters who have always been white. You will take another look at us and say that we are still black and, ethnologically speaking, you will be right. But nationally and culturally, we are as white as the next one. We have put our labor and our blood into the common causes for a long time. We have given the rest of the nation song and laughter. Maybe now, in this terrible struggle, we can give something else—the source and soul of our laughter and song. We offer you our hopebringer, High John de Conquer.

High John de Conquer came to be a man, and a mighty man at that. But he was not a natural man in the beginning. First off, he was a whisper, a will to hope, a wish to find something worthy of laughter and song. Then the whisper put on flesh. His footsteps sounded across the world in a low but musical rhythm as if the world he walked on was a singing-drum. The black folks had an irresistible impulse to laugh. High John de Conquer was a man in full, and had come to live and work on the plantations, and all the slave folks knew him in the flesh.

The sign of this man was a laugh, and his singing-symbol was a drum-beat. No parading drum-shout like soldiers out for show. It did not call to the feet of those who were fixed to hear it. It was an inside thing to live by. It was sure to be heard when and where the work was the hardest, and the lot the most cruel. It helped the slaves endure. They knew that something better was coming. So they laughed in the face of things and sang, "I'm so glad! Trouble don't last always." And the white people who heard them were struck dumb that they could laugh. In an outside way, this was Old Massa's fun, so what was Old Cuffy laughing for?

Old Massa couldn't know, of course, but High John de Conquer was there walking his plantation like a natural man. He was treading the sweat-flavored clods of the plantation, crushing out his drum tunes, and giving out secret laughter. He walked on the winds and moved fast. Maybe he was in Texas when the lash fell on a slave in Alabama, but before the blood was dry on the back he was there. A faint pulsing of a drum like a goat-skin stretched over the heart, that came nearer and closer, then somebody in the saddened quarters would feel like laughing, and say, "Now, High John de Conquer, Old Massa couldn't get the best of him. That old John was a case!" Then everybody sat up and began to smile. Yes, yes, that was right. Old John, High John could beat the unbeatable. He was top-superior to the whole mess of sorrow. He could beat it all, and what made it so cool, finish it off with a laugh. So they pulled the covers up over their souls and kept them from all hurt, harm and danger and made them a laugh and a song. Night time was a joke, because daybreak was on the way. Distance and the impossible had no power over High John de Conquer.

He had come from Africa. He came walking on the waves of sound. Then he took on flesh after he got there. The sea captains of ships knew that they brought slaves in their ships. They knew about those black bodies huddled down there in the middle passage, being hauled across the waters to helplessness. John de Conquer was walking the very winds that filled the sails of the ship. He followed over them like the albatross.

It is no accident that High John de Conquer has evaded the ears of white people. They were not supposed to know. You can't know what folks won't tell you. If they, the white people, heard some scraps, they could not understand because they had nothing to hear things like that with. They were not looking for any hope in those days, and it was not much of a strain for them to find something to laugh over. Old John would have been out of place for them.

Old Massa met our hope-bringer all right, but when Old Massa met him, he was not going by his right name. He was traveling, and touristing around the plantations as the laugh-provoking Brer Rabbit. So Old Massa and Old Miss and their young ones laughed with and at Brer Rabbit and wished him well. And all the time, there was High John de Conquer playing his tricks of making a way out of no-way. Hitting a straight lick with a crooked stick. Winning the jack pot with no other stake but a laugh. Fighting a mighty battle without outside-showing force, and winning his war from within. Really winning in a permanent way, for he was winning with the soul of the black man whole and free. So he could use it afterwards. For what shall it profit a man if he gain the whole world, and lose his own soul? You would have nothing but a cruel, vengeful, grasping monster come to power. John de Conquer was a bottom-fish. He was deep. He had the wisdom tooth of the East in his head. Way over there, where the sun rises a day ahead of time, they say that Heaven arms with love and laughter those it does not wish to see destroyed. He who carries his heart in his sword must perish. So says the ultimate law. High John de Conquer knew a lot of things like that. He who wins from within is in the "Be" class. *Be* here when the ruthless man comes, and *be* here when he is gone.

Moreover, John knew that it is written where it cannot be erased, that nothing shall live on human flesh and prosper. Old Maker said that before He made any more sayings. Even a man-eating tiger and lion can teach a person that much. His flabby muscles and mangy hide can teach an emperor right from wrong. If the emperor would only listen.

II

There is no established picture of what sort of looking-man this John de Conquer was. To some, he was a big, physical-looking man like John Henry. To others, he was a little, hammered-down, low-built man like the Devil's doll-baby. Some said that they never heard what he looked like. Nobody told them, but he lived on the plantation where their old folks were slaves. He is not so well known to the present generation of colored people in the same way that he was in slavery time. Like King Arthur of England, he has served his people, and gone back into mystery again. And, like King Arthur, he is not dead. He waits to return when his people shall call again. Symbolic of English power, Arthur came out of the water, and with Excalibur, went back into the water again. High John de Conquer went back to Africa, but he left his power here, and placed his American dwelling in the root of a certain plant. Only possess that root, and he can be summoned at any time.

"Of course, High John de Conquer got plenty power!" Aunt Shady Anne Sutton bristled at me when I asked her about him. She took her pipe out of her mouth and stared at me out of her deeply wrinkled face. "I hope you ain't one of these here smart colored folks that done got so they don't believe nothing, and come here questionizing me so you can have something to poke fun at. Done got shamed of the things that brought us through. Make out 'tain't no such thing no more."

When I assured her that that was not the case, she went on.

"Sho John de Conquer means power. That's bound to

be so. He come to teach and tell us. God don't leave nobody ignorant, you child. Don't care where He drops you down, He puts you on a notice. He don't want folks taken advantage of because they don't know. Now, back there in slavery time, us didn't have no power of protection, and God knowed it, and put us under watch-care. Rattlesnakes never bite no colored folks until fours years after freedom was declared. That was to give us time to learn and to know. 'Course, I don't know nothing about slavery personal like. I wasn't born till two years after the Big Surrender. Then I wasn't nothing but a infant baby when I was born, so I couldn't know nothing but what they told me. My mama told me, and I know that she wouldn't mislead me, how High John de Conquer helped us out. He had done teached the black folks so they knowed a hundred years ahead of time that freedom was coming. Long before the white folks knowed anything about it at all.

"These young Negroes reads they books and talk about the war freeing the Negroes, but Aye, Lord! A heap sees, but a few knows. 'Course, the war was a help, but how come the war took place? They think they knows, but they don't. John de Conquer had done put it into the white folks to give us our freedom, that's what. Old Massa fought against it, but us could have told him that it wasn't no use. Freedom just had to come. The time set aside for it was there. That war was just a sign and a symbol of the thing. That's the truth! If I tell the truth about everything as good as I do about that, I can go straight to Heaven without a prayer."

Aunt Shady Anne was giving the inside feeling and meaning to the outside laughs around John de Conquer. He romps, he clowns, and looks ridiculous, but if you will, you can read something deeper behind it all. He is loping on off from the Tar Baby with a laugh.

Take, for instance, those words he had with Old Massa about stealing pigs.

Old John was working in Old Massa's house that time, serving around the eating table. Old Massa loved roast pigs, and had them often for dinner. Old John loved them too, but Massa never allowed the slaves to eat any at all. Even put aside the leftover and ate it next time. John de Conquer got tired of that. He took to stopping by the pig pen when he had a strong taste for pigmeat, and getting himself one, and taking it on down to his cabin and cooking it.

Massa began to miss his pigs, and made up his mind to squat for who was taking them and give whoever it was a good hiding. So John kept on taking pigs, and one night Massa walked him down. He stood out there in the dark and saw John kill the pig and went on back to the "big house" and waited till he figured John had it dressed and cooking. Then he went on down to the quarters and knocked on John's door.

"Who dat?" John called out big and bold, because he never dreamed that it was Massa rapping.

"It's me, John," Massa told him. "I want to come in."

"What you want, Massa? I'm coming right out."

"You needn't do that, John. I want to come in."

"Naw, naw, Massa. You don't want to come in no old slave cabin. Youse too fine a man for that. It would hurt my feelings to see you in a place like this here one."

"I tell you I want to come in, John!"

So John had to open the door and let Massa in. John had seasoned that pig down, and it was stinking pretty! John knowed Old Massa couldn't help but smell it. Massa talked on about the crops and hound dogs and one thing and another, and the pot with the pig in it was hanging over the fire in the chimney and kicking up. The smell got better and better.

Way after while, when that pig had done simbled down to a low gravy, Massa said, "John, what's that you cooking in that pot?"

"Nothing but a little old weasly possum, Massa. Sick-liest little old possum I ever did see. But I thought I'd cook him anyhow."

"Get a plate and give me some of it, John. I'm hungry."

"Aw, naw, Massa, you ain't hongry."

"Now, John, I don't mean to argue with you another minute. You give me some of that in the pot, or I mean to have the hide off of your back tomorrow morning. Give it to me!"

So John got up and went and got a plate and a fork and went to the pot. He lifted the lid and looked at Massa and told him, "Well, Massa, I put this thing in here a possum, but if it comes out a pig, it ain't no fault of mine."

Old Massa didn't want to laugh, but he did before he caught himself. He took the plate of brownded down pig and ate it up. He never said nothing, but he gave John and all the other house servants roast pig at the big house after that.

III

John had numerous scrapes and tight squeezes, but he usually came out like Brer Rabbit. Pretty occasionally, though, Old Massa won the hand. The curious thing about this is, that there are no bitter tragic tales at all. When Old Massa won, the thing ended up in a laugh just the same. Laughter at the expense of the slave, but laughter right on. A sort of recognition that life is not one-sided. A sense of humor that said, "We are just as ridiculous as anybody else. We can be wrong, too."

There are many tales, and variants of each, of how the Negro got his freedom through High John de Conquer. The best one deals with a plantation where the work was hard, and Old Massa mean. Even Old Miss used to pull her maids' ears with hot firetongs when they got her riled. So, naturally, Old John de Conquer was around that plantation a lot.

"What we need is a song," he told the people after he had figured the whole thing out. "It ain't here, and it ain't no place I knows of as yet. Us better go hunt around. This has got to be a particular piece of singing."

But the slaves were scared to leave. They knew what Old Massa did for any slave caught running off.

"Oh, Old Massa don't need to know you gone from here. How? Just leave your old work-tired bodies around for him to look at, and he'll never realize youse way off somewhere, going about your business."

At first they wouldn't hear to John, that is, some of them. But, finally, the weak gave in to the strong, and John told them to get ready to go while he went off to get something for them to ride on. They were all gathered up under a big hickory nut tree. It was noon time and they were knocked off from chopping cotton to eat their dinner. And then that tree was right where Old Massa and Old Miss could see from the cool veranda of the big house. And both of them were sitting out there to watch.

"Wait a minute, John. Where we going to get something to wear like that. We can't go nowhere like you talking about dressed like we is."

"Oh, you got plenty things to wear. Just reach inside yourselves and get out all those fine raiments you been toting with you for the last longest. They is in there, all right. I know. Get 'em out, and put 'em on."

So the people began to dress. And then John hollered back for them to get out their musical instruments so they could play music on the way. They were right inside where they got their fine raiments from. So they began to get them out. Nobody remembered that Massa and Miss were sitting up there on the veranda looking things over. So John went off for a minute. After that they all heard a big sing of wings. It was John come back riding on a great black crow. The crow was so big that one wing rested on the morning, while the other dusted off the evening star.

John lighted down and helped them, so they all mounted on, and the bird took out straight across the deep blue sea. But it was a pearly blue, like ten squillion big pearl jewels dissolved in running gold. The shore around it was all grainy gold itself.

Like Jason in search of the golden fleece, John and his party went to many places, and had numerous adventures. They stopped off in Hell where John, under the name of Jack, married the Devil's youngest daughter and became a popular character. So much so, that when he and the Devil had some words because John turned the dampers down in old Original Hell and put some of the Devil's hogs to barbecue over the coals, John ran for High Chief Devil and won the election. The rest of his party was overjoyed at the possession of power and wanted to stay there. But John said no. He reminded them that they had come in search of a song. A song that would whip Old Massa's earlaps down. The song was not in Hell. They must go on.

The party escaped out of Hell behind the Devil's two fast horses. One of them was named Hallowed-Be-Thy-Name, and the other, Thy-Kingdom-Come. They made it to the mountain. Somebody told them that the Golden Stairs went from there. John decided that since they were in the vicinity, they might as well visit Heaven.

They got there a little weary and timid. But the gates swung wide for them, and they went in. They were bathed, robed, and given new and shining instruments to play on. Guitars of gold, and drums, and cymbals and wind-singing instruments. They walked up Amen Avenue, and down Hallelujah Street and found with delight that Amen Avenue was tuned to sing base and alto. The west end was deep bass, and the east end alto. Hallelujah Street was tuned for tenor and soprano, and the two promenades met right in front of the throne and made harmony by themselves. You could make any tune you wanted to by the way you walked. John and his party had a very good time at that and other things. Finally, by the way they acted and did, Old Maker called them up before His great workbench, and made them a tune and put it in their mouths. It had no words. It was a tune that you could bend and shape in most any way you wanted to fit the words and feelings that you had. They learned it and began to sing.

Just about that time a loud rough voice hollered, "You Tunk! You July! You Aunt Diskie!" Then Heaven went black before their eyes and they couldn't see a thing until they saw the hickory nut tree over their heads again. There was everything just like they had left it, with Old Massa and Old Miss sitting on the veranda, and Massa was doing the hollering.

"You all are taking a mighty long time for dinner," Massa said. "Get up from there and get back to the field. I mean for you to finish chopping that cotton today if it takes all night long. I got something else, harder than that, for you to do tomorrow. Get a move on you."

They heard what Massa said, and they felt bad right off. But John de Conquer took and told them saying, "Don't pay what he say no mind. You know where you got something finer than this plantation and anything it's got on it, put away. Ain't that funny? Us got all that, and he don't know nothing at all about it. Don't tell him nothing. Nobody don't have to know where us gets our pleasure from. Come on. Pick up your hoes and let's go."

They all began to laugh and grabbed up their hoes and started out.

"Ain't that funny?" Aunt Diskie laughed and hugged herself with secret laughter. "Us got all the advantage, and Old Massa think he got us tied!"

The crowd broke out singing as they went off to work. The day didn't seem hot like it had before. Their gift song came along into their memories in pieces, and they sang about glittering new robes and harps, and the work flew.

IV

So after a while, freedom came. Therefore High John de Conquer has not walked the winds of America for seventy-five years now. His people had their freedom, their laugh and their song. They have traded it to other Americans for things they could use like education and property, and acceptance. High John knew that that was the way it would be, so he could retire with his secret smile into the soil of the South and wait.

The thousands upon thousands of humble people who still believe in him, that is, in the power of love and laughter to win by their subtle power, do John reverence by getting the root of the plant in which he has taken up his secret dwelling, and "dressing" it with perfume, and keeping it on their person, or in their houses in a secret place. It is there to help them overcome things they feel that they could not beat otherwise, and to bring them the laugh of the day. John will never forsake the weak and the helpless, nor fail to bring hope to the hopeless. That is what they believe, and so they do not worry. They go on and laugh and sing. Things are bound to come out right tomorrow. That is the secret of Negro song and laughter.

So the brother in black offers to these United States the source of courage that endures, and laughter. High John de Conquer. If the news from overseas reads bad, and the nation inside seems like it is stuck in the Tar Baby, listen hard, and you will hear John de Conquer treading on his singing-drum. You will know then, that no matter how bad things look now, it will be worse for those who seek to oppress us.

Even if your hair comes yellow, and your eyes are blue, John de Conquer will be working for you just the same. From his secret place, he is working for all America now. We are all his kinfolks. Just be sure our cause is right, and then you can lean back and say, "John de Conquer would know what to do in a case like this, and then he would finish it off with a laugh."

White America, take a laugh out of our black mouths, and win! We give you High John de Conquer.

Paul Bunyan Stories

Davy Crockett and James Bowie were historical characters whose exploits became part of oral tradition. Paul Bunyan, on the other hand, owes his popularity to gifted storytellers who anticipated America's need for a superhuman hero capable of felling entire forests with a single stroke. This personification of pure power influenced many American writers, including Carl Sandburg, whose reverence for Americana misled him into accepting Bunyan as a true creation of the people.

PAUL BUNYAN
by Carl Sandburg

I. WHO MADE PAUL BUNYAN?

Who made Paul Bunyan, who gave him birth as a myth, who joked him into life as the Master Lumberjack, who fashioned him forth as an apparition easing the hours of men amid axes and trees, saws and lumber? The people, the book-less people, they made Paul and had him alive long before he got into the books for those who read. He grew up in shanties,

around the hot stoves of winter, among socks and mittens dry-
ing, in the smell of tobacco smoke and the roar of laughter
mocking the outside weather. And some of Paul came overseas
in wooden bunks below decks in sailing vessels. And some of
Paul is old as the hills, young as the alphabet.

The Pacific Ocean froze over in the winter of the Blue
Snow and Paul Bunyan had long teams of oxen hauling regular white snow over from China. This was the winter Paul gave
a party to the Seven Axmen. Paul fixed a granite floor sunk
two hundred feet deep for them to dance on. Still, it tipped
and tilted as the dance went on. And because the Seven Axmen refused to take off their hob-nailed boots, the sparks from
the nails of their dancing feet lit up the place so that Paul
didn't light the kerosene lamps. No women being on the Big
Onion river at that time the Seven Axmen had to dance with
each other, the one left over in each set taking Paul as a part-
ner. The commotion of the dancing that night brought on an
earthquake and the Big Onion river moved over three counties
to the east.

One year when it rained from St. Patrick's Day till the
Fourth of July, Paul Bunyan got disgusted because his cele-
bration of the Fourth was spoiled. He dived into Lake Superior
and swam to where a solid pillar of water was coming down.
He dived under this pillar, swam up into it and climbed with
powerful swimming strokes, was gone about an hour, came
splashing down, and as the rain stopped, he explained, "I
turned the dam thing off." This is told in the Big North Woods
and on the Great Lakes, with many particulars.

Two mosquitoes lighted on one of Paul Bunyan's oxen,
killed it, ate it, cleaned the bones, and sat on a grub shanty
picking their teeth as Paul came along. Paul sent to Australia
for two special bumble bees to kill these mosquitoes. But the
bees and the mosquitoes intermarried; their children had sting-
ers on both ends. And things kept getting worse till Paul
brought a big boatload of sorghum up from Louisiana and

while all the bee-mosquitoes were eating at the sweet sorghum he floated them down to the Gulf of Mexico. They got so fat that it was easy to drown them all between New Orleans and Galveston.

Paul logged on the Little Gimlet in Oregon one winter. The cook stove at that camp covered an acre of ground. They fastened the side of a hog on each snowshoe and four men used to skate on the griddle while the cook flipped the pancakes. The eating table was three miles long; elevators carried the cakes to the ends of the table where boys on bicycles rode back and forth on a path down the center of the table dropping the cakes where called for.

Benny, the Little Blue Ox of Paul Bunyan, grew two feet every time Paul looked at him, when a youngster. The barn was gone one morning and they found it on Benny's back; he grew out of it in a night. One night he kept pawing and bellowing for more pancakes, till there were two hundred men at the cook shanty stove trying to keep him fed. About breakfast time Benny broke loose, tore down the cook shanty, ate all the pancakes piled up for the loggers' breakfast. After that Benny made his mistake; he ate the red hot stove; and that finished him. This is only one of the hot stove stories told in the North Woods.

THE BEDCATS

by Glen Rounds

Ol' Paul had quite a time with the Bedcats one winter, when he was using one of his old camps that had stood deserted for thirty years or more. It happened this way. As every one knows, most bunkhouses have a certain number of bedbugs. These don't annoy a real lumberjack to amount to anything, although you'll hear the greenhorns holler plenty when they first come into camp. But they either make friends with the little beasts or they don't last long. The story is that the loggers all had their pet bugs that followed them around camp and out in the woods like dogs, some even being trained, it is said, to steal blankets off adjoining bunks for their masters on especially cold nights. However, that is as it may be; I never saw it.

But it is a well-known fact that the intelligent little beasts always knew when camp was to be moved, and the night before would come out of wherever they were in the habit of staying and climb into the bedding rolls so as not to be left behind. Then when the new camp was set up, there they were, jumping up and down with excitement to greet the men when they came in from their first day's work.

One time, though, they got fooled. That was the time the Indian, Squatting Calf, comes running into camp just after breakfast with the news that gold has been discovered in the Black Hills. Right away all the men tear out over the hills without even waiting to pick up their blankets. Within three minutes the camp is as empty as an old maid's letter box on Valentine's Day. That night at sundown the little bugs are all lined up at the bunkhouse door waiting for the men to come home as usual. But they don't come.

Ol' Paul's in town at the time, and when he hears the news, he knows there's no use figuring on logging till the gold fever passes, so he goes on a timber cruising trip. He locates some fine timber down Kansas way, and when he finds his men ready to work, he starts a new camp there, as he has a ready market for his lumber in the new gold towns. And, what with one thing and another, it's about thirty years before he comes back to the old camp. But when he does, he finds trouble waiting for him.

He and the men get there about noon and start cleaning out the old buildings. They're a little surprised to find the bunks filled up with the bones of rabbits and other small animals, but suppose that owls or bobcats have been living there. By night the camp is ready, and after supper the men turn in early. Ol' Paul suddenly wakes up, hearing wild yells and snarls from the bunkhouse, and comes running out of his office to see the men clawing over one another in their underwear, trying to get out in the open. They swear that their bunks are full of wildcats which have been crawling all over them. Now Paul knows wildcats, and he's never heard of one that'll come within a hundred yards of a logger if it has its 'druthers. As he can find nothing in there when he looks, he figures that being as it's the day after payday, the men have probably eaten something that disagrees with them. But they won't go back in the bunkhouse, so he lets them sleep in the stables that night.

But the next night the same thing happens, so Paul decides to get his pistol and sleep in the bunkhouse himself. When a bunch of lumberjacks are scared to sleep in a place there must be something wrong somewhere. For a time things are quiet enough to suit anybody, and Paul finally decides that the men have been reading too many old mystery magazines, and dozes off. But he wakes up mighty soon. What feels like a couple of full-grown wildcats seem to have gotten tangled up in his beard, and his blanket is heaving around like he has a runaway cat show under it. The whole bunk is full of animals of some kind, hissing and snarling like all get out. It's none too comfortable there, but Ol' Paul doesn't lose his head. He grabs out in the dark and gets a couple of the beasts and stuffs them into a sack he's got handy. Of course as soon as he starts floundering around the things clear out, like any wild animal, and by the time the men come running with lanterns the place is quiet again.

They carefully open up the sack to see what they're caught. The animals inside are not bobcats, but they have several pairs of legs. They are covered with a heavy coat of reddish-brown fur, which is quite long on the back, but due to the shortness of their legs, is worn down to the length of plush on the bottom. Naturally Paul and the men are more than a little puzzled.

It is not until the Indians come into camp that they find out what it is they have caught. The Indians call them Bedcats, and from them Paul learns the story.

It seems that the little bugs, being left alone in camp, had to forage for themselves. At first many died, but the stronger ones survived and grew larger, soon attacking small mice and sparrows. As the years passed, they grew fur to keep them warm, and became more and more savage, each generation a little larger and wilder than the one before. Eventually they were bringing in gophers and small rabbits to feed their young. Later, it seems, they crossed with bobcats and the half-breeds were really fierce hunters. They took to running in packs like wolves, baying at the moon, and in a pitched fight a full-grown bobcat was no match for even an ordinary-sized Bedcat. The Indians set deadfalls for them, and made warm fur robes and mittens from the pelts. But with the return of the lumberjacks, some forgotten instinct seemed to urge them into the blankets in the bunks, which upset even the soundest sleepers.

Something had to be done. Ol' Paul buys the Indians a lot of number four wolf traps and offers a five-dollar bounty for the scalps, so they are soon trapped out. I haven't heard of any quite that big being seen since.

PIPELINE DAYS AND PAUL BUNYAN
by Ancel Garland

It was evening. The sun hung like a sandy ball above the rim of dull mesquite that surrounded the pipeline camp. For three weeks the line had been extending through a lifeless country of mesquite and dust. For three weeks the men had been broiling under the August sun with not even a wind to make the heat less deadening. Now they were sprawled on the grass in easy after-supper positions. Forming a half circle about the cook shack, they rested uncomfortably and "razzed" the lone fat man who had not yet finished eating. "Fat" was always last—last to start work, last to stop eating, and certainly last to stop talking. "Fat" ate on, unconcerned with their tired humor. Gradually the men drifted into small groups and lay droning a preparation for the evening's talk.

"Git a scoop. That's what you need, Fat."

"Move the chuck wagon and he'll starve to death. He's too damn lazy to follow it."

"Hey, Fat, did you ever get all you wanted to eat?"

"They ought to grow square beans so he could get more of them on his knife."

"Talk about eating. Tell you what I saw once," said one who aspired to Fat's position as the camp's chief liar. "I saw a man eat a whole ham once—well, not exactly a whole ham, we had eaten a meal off it—not exactly we, my brother-in-law Jim and his family. The man came to the house one morning and wanted something to eat. Sis was busy and didn't have time to be fooling with him; so she just set the table and put this ham on it and then went on about her housework or whatever she was doing. Well, when she came back the man was gone and so was the ham—all except the bone and it had been gnawed so dry that even the dog wouldn't touch it. That's the God's truth. Jim swears it's the truth."

The men howled derisively, and Fat, who had been listening half attentively, arose from his stool and sauntered into the center of the group.

"Did you say something about eating?" he said. "Well I had a funny thing happen to me the other day in Wichita Falls. I goes into one of them restaurants down by the railroad tracks to eat. When I come in I saw a couple of tough hombres setting at the counter and they looks me over kind of amused like. But I goes on back and sets down a couple of seats from them. After a while the waiter comes out from behind and goes over to where they are setting and asks them what they want.

"They was sure tough-looking birds, and one of them speaks up and says, 'Gimme a T-bone steak a inch and a quarter thick. Just scorch it.' And he looks over at me kinda mean like.

"But I didn't pay him no mind but just set there. So the other one pulls his hat 'way down over his eye, and says, 'Gimme a hind quarter. Raw.' And then they both looks over at me.

"Well, when the waiter come over to where I am setting, I says to him, 'Gimme a sharp butcher knife and then just cripple a steer and run him through here. I'll cut off what I want!' "

"Speaking of steers," the Contender put in, "did you ever hear about the cattle line that Paul Bunyan laid down from his ranch to Chicago?

"Well, Paul he got tired of paying such high freight to get his stock to market; so he just laid a pipeline all the way to the stockyards in Chicago and pumped them through it. Everything went all right except that the pipe was so big that the calves and half-grown yearlin's would get lost in the threads and starve to death before they could get to the outside. And one time the line sprung a leak and Paul lost thirty-five carloads of cattle before he could get it corked [caulked]. But he sure did do a good job of corking when he did get to it."

"How the devil did he cork a hole that big?" asked Fat after a minute or two of silence.

"Why with B. S., you big windbag, same as that that you have been spouting off."

Fat sat for a moment trying to think of a way to get "back at" the Contender. Then he started off on a new trail.

"You know so much about Paul Bunyan," he said. "Did you ever hear about that big steer he had? He called her Babe and she just measured forty-two pick-handles lengths and the width of a size seven derby hat between the eyes. And strong! Why that steer could pull anything!

"I remember one time when we was drilling a well down Breckenridge way. Wasn't much of a hole, just sixteen inches. Well, we drilled and drilled and didn't ever strike nothing— except dust, and a God's plenty of that; so finally Paul he said we might as well give it up as a dry hole and let it go at that.

"But Paul was mad! He swore around for two or three days and smashed the derrick into kindling wood and was about to quit drilling when he saw a advertisement in the paper by some bird out on the plains that wanted to buy some post-holes. Ten thousand post holes it was he wanted. Ten thousand holes three feet long.

"Well, Paul he hitched a chain around this duster hole and hooked up Babe and pulled fifteen thousand feet of it out of the ground. He got mad again because the hole broke off and left over half of it in the ground. But directly he said that they wasn't no use of a post hole being sixteen inches across; so he just quartered the hole and then sawed it up into the right lengths.

"You know out on the plains they have a awful hard time digging post holes, or any other kind of holes for that matter. The soil out there is only a foot deep till you strike solid rock and they can't dig through this rock a-tall.

"Why them guys used to come down into East Texas and buy all the old wells and dug-outs that they could get a-hold of and cut them up to use for post holes. I used to know a feller down there that could dig and stack on cars more old wells than any man I ever saw before. He could stack twenty-nine of them on cars in a day and take two hours off for dinner.

"They finally moved so many wells from down there that they ruined the water; so they was a ordinance passed against it. But that didn't stop it. They bootlegged them out to the plains. I knew one guy that got rich bootlegging them. He had a patented jack that would lift a well or a dug-out right out of the ground.

"It don't do much good to build fences out on the plains, though. That there wind out there is awful. Soon as a man gets a good fence built, along comes the wind and blows it away, posts, post holes, and all. Why, that wind even blows wells away and a guy told me that he seen it turn prairie dog holes wrong side out it blew so hard. But I never did believe it. Them guys are awful liars. One of them told me he had a horse throw him so high one time that he had to catch a-holt of a cloud to keep from falling and killing himself. It's cold out there too—"

"I'll says it is," a pipeliner broke in. "Like that guy that was up in Canada somewheres when it was fifty degrees below. He come up to another guy and said, 'God, man, wouldn't you hate to be in Amarillo today?' "

"Ja ever hear about them wells out in Colorado where the oil freezes when it comes out of the ground?" asked the Contender. "They can't pipe it away; so they just let it spout out on the ground and then shovel it into wagons with scoops and haul it off."

"That's like some of them wells that Paul Bunyan drilled in over at Smackover," said someone. "They was gushers and blew in so strong that they had to put roofs over the derricks to keep the oil from spouting a hole in the sky."

"I worked for Paul out in Arizona on the biggest well that I ever worked on," resumed the Contender. "It was a seventy-five-inch hole, it was, and we had to make a derrick so tall that it had to be hinged in two places and folded up before the sun and stars could pass. Took a man fourteen days to climb to the top of it. It did. And Paul had to hire thirty derrick men so we could have a man on top all of the time. They was always fourteen men going up and fourteen men coming down, a man on top and a man off tower,[1] all the time. And they was dog houses built a day's climbing apart for the men to sleep in while they was going up and down.

"Why, when that well blew in, it took three days for the oil to reach the top of the derrick, and it rained oil for a week after we had got it capped.

"It was some well. We drilled it with one of Paul's patented rotary rigs. Never could have drilled so deep—it was sixty thousand feet—if Paul hadn't used flexible drill pipe. We just wound the drill stem up on the draw-works. Take a devil of a long time to come out of the hole if we had had to stack it.

"Well, when we was down sixty thousand and three feet, the well blew in. And when we had come out of the hole we seen that we had forgot to case it. Well, Paul he called out both towers and made up the casing on the ground—about ten miles of seventy-five-inch casing—and then he just picked it up and dropped it down into place."

"I worked for Paul on one of them deep wells once," said Fat. "It was out in Arkansas. Jimmy Blue was running the rig and we was drilling with standard tools. We got down thirty thousand feet and struck a rock formation that a bit wouldn't touch. And we was using a pretty good sized bit too, drilling a fifty-inch hole.

"Well, we worked on this formation for three weeks without doing any good and then we called up Paul. Paul he come out and took charge of the rig himself and worked for three more weeks, day and night, without doing anything except ruin a lot of bits. And finally he got so mad that he jumped down on the derrick floor and pulled up the bit with his hands. Then he threw it down into the holes as hard as he could throw

---

[1] The reader may take his choice of spellings: "tower" or "tour." The word is pronounced "tower," and means a shift of men. The drilling crews work in two towers of twelve hours each, from twelve o'clock to twelve. The tower that goes on at midnight is the "graveyard tower," the one that goes at noon is the "gravy tower."—A. G.

it. Well, we busted the rock that time. The bit just kept on going and when the line run out it pulled derrick, rig, and all into the hole after it.

"We got a gusher that time. But when Paul seen that the rig had pulled Jimmy into the hole with it he was just about to plug off the hole and abandon it. But in a few days we got a telegram from Jimmy in China saying that he had a 100,000 barrel gusher and was spudding in on another location."

"Did any of you guys work for Paul on that big line he laid?" asked the Contender. "Well, I worked for him on that 101-inch aluminum line that he laid from Pennsylvania to California. We laid it to pipe buttermilk out to his camp out there. Paul liked buttermilk so well himself that he had a twenty-four-inch petcock running wide open all the time to catch enough for him to drink."

"Yeh," said Fat, "I know all about that. I helped Paul drill the buttermilk well that furnished that line. We drilled down thirty-two thousand feet and then struck a formation of cornbread. We drilled for five hundred feet through the cornbread and then for twelve hundred feet through solid turnip greens—except that every few feet would be a layer of fried sow-belly. That's where the old song started: 'Cornbread, Buttermilk, and Good Old Turnip Greens.' "

"Fat, did you ever see Paul's wife?" asked a young boll-weevil who had started to work only a few days before. "She had a wooden leg and she was so homely that we used to scrape enough ugly off her face every day to mud off a well. The hardest six months' work I ever put in was painting that wooden leg of hers."

"When Paul worked on the highlines he had a wooden leg himself," added an ex-linesman. "It was ninety feet long and the men used to wear one out every three days climbing up to bum him for cigarettes."

"Paul discovered perpetual motion—of the jaw—when he got Fat to work for him," said the Contender.

"Huh," said Fat, "the only perpetual motion Paul ever discovered was one time down in India. We was drilling a ninety-inch hole with standard tools. And when we got down twenty-seven thousand feet we struck the root of a rubber tree and the bit never did stop bouncing. Had to abandon the hole."

"I worked—" the Contender began.

"Yeh, and on another one of them wells we was drilling a eighty-inch offset. Had them big derricks all around us. And our camp was setting so far back in them derricks that we had to pipe the daylight in. We drilled down nearly fifty thousand feet and struck a flowing vein of alum water and the hole, rig, and everything drew up until we had to abandon it."

"Paul sure had drilling down to a fine point," said the Contender. "Why I worked for him on one hole where we was using rubber tools. We would just start the tools bouncing and then go to sleep until it was time to change the bit. And the men was so fast that the driller would just bounce the bit out of the hole and they would change it before it could fall back."

"Paul's camp wasn't nothing like this dump," said Fat. "I worked for him on a ninety-inch line once and we had so many men in the camp that it took fifteen adding machines running day and night to keep track of their time. Paul invented the first ditching machine while we was laying this line through Arkansas. He bought a drove of them razorback hogs and trained them to root in a straight line."

"You telling about that cattle line of Paul's a while back reminds me of the trees that used to grow down on the Brazos," said the "Old Man." "One time I was working through that country with a herd of cattle and come up to the river where I couldn't ford it. While I was setting on my horse looking at the water I heard a big crash up the river and when I went up to see what it was, it was a tree had fallen across the river. It was one of them big holler trees. So I just drove my herd across the river through the holler of it. But when I got to the other side and counted the herd I seen that they was nearly three hundred steers missing and I went back to look for them. They had wandered off into the limbs and got lost."

"That reminds me of the sand storms that they used to have down in East Texas," said the Contender. "One time they was a Negro riding along one of them sandy roads on a jackass and he stopped to go down to the creek and get a drink and tied his mule to a sapling by the side of the road. While he was gone it come one of them sand storms and when he come back he seen his ass hanging by the tie-rope about seventy feet up in a tree. The sand had blown away from under him and just left him hanging there."

"Say," said Fat, "did any of you guys ever see Paul Bunyan in a poker game? The cards he used were so big that it took a man five hours to walk around one of them. Paul used to play a lot of poker that time we was digging Lake Michigan to mix concrete in when he was building the Rocky Mountains. A little while after that we dug Lake Superior for a slush pit for one of them big wells we was drilling. Any of you birds want to play some poker?"

This, from Fat, was the signal for retiring. The sun was long past set and mosquitoes were buzzing in the darkened mesquite. Silently the men stalked off toward their tents—all except two or three who followed Fat to his tent for a session at poker.

THE SAGA OF PECOS BILL
by Edward O'Reilly

Like Paul Bunyan, Pecos Bill was created by professional writers who sensed a popular need, in this case for a cowboy demigod.

Despite his doubtful origins, he has come to be considered a true folk hero by Americans. This selection is a good summary of Pecos Bill's career.

It is highly probable that Paul Bunyan, whose exploits were told in a recent number of *The Century Magazine,* and Pecos Bill, mythical cowboy hero of the Southwest, were blood brothers. At all events, they can meet on one common ground: they were both fathered by a liar.

Pecos Bill is not a newcomer in the Southwest. His mighty deeds have been sung for generations by the men of the range. In my boyhood days in west Texas I first heard of Bill, and in later years I have often listened to chapters of his history told around the chuck wagon by gravely mendacious cowboys.

The stranger in cattle land usually hears of Bill if he shows an incautious curiosity about the cow business. Some old-timer is sure to remark mournfully:

"Ranchin' ain't what it was in the days Bill staked out New Mexico."

If the visitor walks into the trap and inquires further about Bill, he is sure to receive an assortment of misinformation that every cowhand delights in unloading on the unwary.

Although Bill has been quoted in a number of Western stories, the real history of his wondrous deeds has never been printed. I have here collected a few of the tales about him which will doubtless be familiar to cowmen, but deserve to be passed on to a larger audience.

Bill invented most of the things connected with the cow business. He was a mighty man of valor, the king killer of the bad men, and it was Bill who taught the broncho how to buck. It is a matter of record that he dug the Rio Grande one dry year when he grew tired of packin' water from the Gulf of Mexico.

According to the most veracious historians, Bill was born

about the time Sam Houston discovered Texas. His mother was a sturdy pioneer woman who once killed forty-five Indians with a broom handle, and weaned him on moonshine liquor when he was three days old. He cut his teeth on a bowie knife, and his earliest playfellows were the bears and catamounts of east Texas.

When Bill was about a year old, another family moved into the country, and located about fifty miles down the river. His father decided the place was gettin' too crowded, and packed his family in a wagon and headed west.

One day after they crossed the Pecos River, Bill fell out of the wagon. As there were sixteen or seventeen other children in the family, his parents didn't miss him for four or five weeks, and then it was too late to try to find him.

That's how Bill came to grow up with the coyotes along the Pecos. He soon learned the coyote language, and used to hunt with them and sit on the hills and howl at night. Being so young when he got lost, he always thought he was a coyote. That's where he learned to kill deer by runnin' them to death.

One day when he was about ten years old a cowboy came along just when Bill had matched a fight with two grizzly bears. Bill hugged the bears to death, tore off a hind leg, and was just settin' down to breakfast when this cowboy loped up and asked him what he meant by runnin' around naked that way among the varmints.

"Why, because I am a varmint," Bill told him. "I'm a coyote."

The cowboy argued with him that he was a human, but Bill wouldn't believe him.

"Ain't I got fleas?" he insisted. "And don't I howl around all night, like a respectable coyote should do?"

"That don't prove nothin'," the cowboy answered. "All Texans have fleas, and most of them howl. Did you ever see a coyote that didn't have a tail? Well, you ain't got no tail; so that proves you ain't a varmint."

Bill looked, and sure enough, he didn't have a tail.

"You sure got me out on a limb," says Bill. "I never noticed that before. It shows what higher education will do for a man. I believe you're right. Lead me to them humans, and I'll throw in with them."

Bill went to town with this cowhand, and in due time he got to enjoyin' all the pleasant vices of mankind, and decided that he certainly was a human. He got to runnin' with the wild bunch, and sunk lower and lower, until finally he became a cowboy.

It wasn't long until he was famous as a bad man. He invented the six-shooter and train-robbin' and most of the crimes popular in the old days of the West. He didn't invent cow-stealin'. That was discovered by King David in the Bible, but Bill improved on it.

There is no way of tellin' just how many men Bill did kill. Deep down he had a tender heart, however, and never killed women or children, or tourists out of season. He never scalped his victims; he was too civilized for that. He used to skin them gently and tan their hides.

It wasn't long before Bill had killed all the bad men in west Texas, massacred all the Indians, and eat all the buffalo. So he decided to migrate to a new country where hard men still thrived and a man could pass the time away.

He saddled up his horse and hit for the West. One day he met an old trapper and told him what he was lookin' for.

"I want the hardest cow outfit in the world," he says. "Not one of these ordinary cow-stealin', Mexican-shootin' bunches of amateurs, but a real hard herd of hand-picked hellions that make murder a fine art and take some proper pride in their slaughter."

"Stranger, you're headed in the right direction," answers the trapper. "Keep right on down this draw for a couple of hundred miles, and you'll find that very outfit. They're so hard they can kick fire out of a flint rock with their bare toes."

Bill single-footed down that draw for about a hundred miles that afternoon; then he met with an accident. His horse stubbed his toe on a mountain and broke his leg, leavin' Bill afoot.

He slung his saddle over his shoulder and set off hikin' down that draw, cussin' and a-swearin'. Profanity was a gift with Bill.

All at once a big ten-foot rattlesnake quiled up in his path, set his tail to singin', and allowed he'd like to match a fight. Bill laid down his saddle, and just to be fair about it, he gave the snake the first three bites. Then he waded into that reptile and everlastingly frailed the pizen out of him.

By and by that old rattler yelled for mercy, and admitted that when it came to fightin', Bill started where he let off. So Bill picked up his saddle and started on, carryin' the snake in his hand and spinnin' it in short loops at the Gila monsters.

About fifty miles further on, a big old mountain lion jumped off a cliff and lit all spraddled out on Bill's neck. This was no ordinary lion. It weighed more than three steers and a yearlin', and was the very same lion the State of Nuevo León was named after down in old Mexico.

Kind of chucklin' to himself, Bill laid down his saddle and his snake and went into action. In a minute the fur was flyin' down the cañon until it darkened the sun. The way Bill knocked the animosity out of that lion was a shame. In about three minutes that lion hollered:

"I'll give up, Bill. Can't you take a joke?"

Bill let him up, and then he cinched the saddle on him and went down that cañon whoopin' and yellin', ridin' that lion a hundred feet a jump, and quirtin' him down the flank with the rattlesnake.

It wasn't long before he saw a chuck wagon with a bunch of cowboys squattin' around it. He rode up to that wagon, splittin' the air with his war whoops, with that old lion a-screechin', and that snake singin' his rattles.

When he came to the fire he grabbed the old cougar by the ear, jerked him back on his haunches, stepped off him, hung his snake around his neck, and looked the outfit over. Them cowboys sat there sayin' less than nothin'.

Bill was hungry, and seein' a boilerful of beans cookin' on the fire, he scooped up a few handfuls and swallowed them, washin' them down with a few gallons of boilin' coffee out of the pot. Wipin' his mouth on a handful of prickly-pear cactus, Bill turned to the cowboys and asked:

"Who the hell is boss around here?"

A big fellow about eight feet tall, with seven pistols and nine bowie-knives in his belt, rose up and, takin' off his hat, said:

"Stranger, I was; but you be."

Bill had many adventures with this outfit. It was about this time he staked out New Mexico, and used Arizona for a calf pasture. It was here that he found his noted horse Widow-Maker. He raised him from a colt on nitroglycerin and dyna-mite, and Bill was the only man that could throw a leg over him.

There wasn't anythin' that Bill couldn't ride, although I have heard of one occasion when he was thrown. He made a bet that he could ride an Oklahoma cyclone slick-heeled, without a saddle.

He met the cyclone, the worst that was ever known, up on the Kansas line. Bill eared that tornado down and climbed on its back. That cyclone did some pitchin' that is unbeliev-able, if it were not vouched for by many reliable witnesses.

Down across Texas, it went sunfishin', back-flippin', side-windin', knockin' down mountains, blowin' the holes out of the ground, and tyin' rivers into knots. The Staked Plains used to be heavily timbered until that big wind swiped the trees off and left it a bare prairie.

Bill just sat there, thumbin' that cyclone in the withers, floppin' it across the ears with his hat, and rollin' a cigarette with one hand. He rode it through three States, but over Arizona it got him.

When it saw it couldn't throw him, it rained out from under him. This is proved by the fact that it washed out the Grand Cañon. Bill came down over in California. The spot where he lit is now known as Death Valley, a hole in the ground more than one hundred feet below sea level, and the print of his hip pockets can still be seen in the granite.

I have heard this story disputed in some of its details. Some historians claim that Bill wasn't thrown; that he slid down on a streak of lightnin' without knockin' the ashes off his cigarette. It is also claimed that the Grand Cañon was dug by Bill one week when he went prospectin'; but the best authorities insist on the first version. They argue that that streak of lightnin' story comes from the habit he always had of usin' one to light his cigarette.

Bill was a great roper. In fact, he invented ropin'. Old-timers who admit they knew him say that his rope was as long as the equator, although the more conservative say that it was at least two feet shorter on one end. He used to rope a herd of cattle at one throw.

This skill once saved the life of a friend. The friend had tried to ride Widow-Maker one day, and was thrown so high he came down on top of Pikes Peak. He was in the middle of a bad fix, because he couldn't get down, and seemed doomed to a lingerin' death on high.

Bill came to the rescue, and usin' only a short calf loop, he roped his friend around the neck and jerked him down to safety in the valley, twenty thousand feet below. This man was always grateful, and became Bill's horse-wrangler at the time he staked out New Mexico.

In his idle moments in New Mexico Bill amused himself puttin' thorns on the trees and horns on the toads. It was on this ranch he dug the Rio Grande and invented the centipede and the tarantula as a joke on his friends.

When the cow business was dull, Pecos Bill occasionally embarked in other ventures; for instance, at one time he took a contract to supply the S. P. Railroad with wood. He hired a few hundred Mexicans to chop and haul the wood to the railroad line. As pay for the job, Bill gave each Mexican one fourth of the wood he hauled.

These Mexicans are funny people. After they received their share of the wood they didn't know what to do with it; so Bill took it off their hands and never charged them a cent.

On another occasion Bill took the job of buildin' the line fence that forms the boundary from El Paso across to the Pacific. He rounded up a herd of prairie dogs and set them to dig holes, which by nature a prairie dog likes to do.

Whenever one of them finished a nice hole and settled down to live in it, Bill evicted him and stuck a fence post in the hole. Everbody admired his foresight except the prairie dogs, and who cares what a prairie dog thinks?

Old Bill was always a very truthful man. To prove this, the cowboys repeat one of his stories, which Bill claimed happened to him. Nobody ever disputed him; that is, no one who is alive now.

He threw in with a bunch of Kiowa Indians one time on a little huntin'-trip. It was about the time the buffalo were getting scarce, and Bill was huntin' with his famous squatter hound named Norther.

Norther would run down a buffalo and hold him by the ear until Bill came up and skinned him alive. Then he would turn it loose to grow a new hide. The scheme worked all right in the summer, but in the winter most of them caught colds and died.

The stories of Bill's love affairs are especially numerous. One of them may be told. It is the sad tale of the fate of his bride, a winsome little maiden called Slue-Foot Sue. She was a famous rider herself, and Bill lost his heart when he saw her riding a catfish down the Rio Grande with only a surcingle.

You must remember that the catfish in the Rio Grande are bigger than whales and twice as active.

Sue made a sad mistake, however, when she insisted on ridin' Widow-Maker on her weddin' day. The old horse threw her so high she had to duck her head to let the moon go by. Unfortunately, she was wearin' her weddin'-gown, and in those days the women wore those big steel-spring bustles.

Well, when Sue lit, she naturally bounced, and every time she came down she bounced again. It was an awful sad sight to see Bill implorin' her to quit her bouncin' and not be so nervous; but Sue kept right on, up and down, weepin', and throwin' kisses to her distracted lover, and carryin' on as a bride naturally would do under those circumstances.

She bounced for three days and four nights, and Bill finally had to shoot her to keep her from starvin' to death. It was mighty tragic. Bill never got over it. Of course he married lots of women after that. In fact, it was one of his weaknesses; but none of them filled the place in his heart once held by Slue-Foot Sue, his bouncin' bride.

There is a great difference of opinion as to the manner of Bill's demise. Many claim that it was his drinkin' habits that killed him. You see, Bill got so that liquor didn't have any kick for him, and he fell into the habit of drinkin' strychnine and other forms of wolf pizen.

Even the wolf bait lost its effect, and he got to puttin' fishhooks and barbed wire in his toddy. It was the barbed wire that finally killed him. It rusted his interior and gave him indigestion. He wasted away to a mere skeleton, weighin' not more than two tons; then up and died, and went to his infernal reward.

Many of the border bards who knew Pecos Bill at his best have a different account of his death.

They say that he met a man from Boston one day, wearing a mail-order cowboy outfit, and askin' fool questions about the West; and poor old Bill laid down and laughed himself to death.

THE BALLAD OF WILLIAM SYCAMORE
by Stephen Vincent Benét

Stephen Vincent Benét, best known for his short story "The Devil and Daniel Webster," created this musical ballad about a frontiersman who represents the pioneering spirit of America. Unfortunately, as the final stanzas point out, the pioneering spirit was often incompatible with the civilization which followed close behind it.

My father, he was a mountaineer,
His fist was a knotty hammer;
He was quick on his feet as a running deer,
And he spoke with a Yankee stammer.

My mother, she was merry and brave,
And so she came to her labor,
With a tall green fir for her doctor grave
And a stream for her comforting neighbor.

And some are wrapped in the linen fine,
And some like a godling's scion;
But I was cradled on twigs of pine
In the skin of a mountain lion.

And some remember a white, starched lap
And a ewer with silver handles;
But I remember a coonskin cap
And the smell of bayberry candles.

The cabin logs, with the bark still rough,
And my mother who laughed at trifles,
And the tall, lank visitors, brown as snuff,
With their long, straight squirrel rifles.

I can hear them dance, like a foggy song,
Through the deepest one of my slumbers,
The fiddle squeaking the boots along
And my father calling the numbers.

The quick feet shaking the puncheon floor,
And the fiddle squealing and squealing,
Till the dried herbs rattled above the door
And the dust went up to the ceiling.

There are children lucky from dawn till dusk,
But never a child so lucky!
For I cut my teeth on "Money Musk"
In the Bloody Ground of Kentucky!

When I grew tall as the Indian corn,
My father had little to lend me,
But he gave me his great, old powder horn
And his woodsman's skill to befriend me.

With a leather shirt to cover my back,
And a redskin nose to unravel
Each forest sign, I carried my pack
As far as a scout could travel.

Till I lost my boyhood and found my wife,
A girl like a Salem clipper!
A woman straight as a hunting knife
With eyes as bright as the Dipper!

We cleared our camp where the buffalo feed,
Unheard-of streams were our flagons;
And I sowed my sons like the apple seed
On the trail of the Western wagons.

They were right, tight boys, never sulky or slow,
A fruitful, a goodly muster.
The eldest died at the Alamo.
The youngest fell with Custer.

The letter that told it burned my hand.
Yet we smiled and said, "So be it!"
But I could not live when they fenced the land
For it broke my heart to see it.

I saddled a red, unbroken colt
And rode him into the day there;
And he threw me down like a thunderbolt
And rolled on me as I lay there.

The hunter's whistle hummed in my ear
As the city men tried to move me,
And I died in my boots like a pioneer
With the whole wide sky above me.

Now I lie in the heart of the fat, black soil,
Like the seed of a prairie thistle;
It has washed my bones with honey and oil
And picked them clean as a whistle.

And my youth returns, like the rains of Spring,
And my sons, like the wild geese flying;
And I lie and hear the meadow lark sing
And have much content in my dying.

Go play with the towns you have built of blocks,
The towns where you would have bound me!
I sleep in my earth like a tired fox,
And my buffalo have found me.

IV. Heroes, Real and Legendary

TALKING IT OVER

1. What character traits does Mobile Jones, in "The Waving of the Spectral Arms," possess that make him a folk hero? Why doesn't West qualify?

2. a) What is there about Davy Crockett in these stories that shows a very human side?
   b) Describe the characteristics of the stereotyped "backwoods braggart" or "ring-tailed roarer" created by Crockett and others. Why do you think such an obviously exaggerated character became popular in the civilized East?
   c) Comment on the strange vocabulary used by Crockett in these tales. Do you think it added to the effectiveness of the stories?

3. a) Jim Bowie is obviously very different from Davy Crockett, yet both are considered folk heroes. Compare and contrast the two.
   b) What legendary English folk hero does Bowie resemble in this story? Compare them.

4. Why is "Mike Fink and the Kicking Sheriff" a humorous story, considering that it describes how one man is severely beaten by another?

5. Why did the Negro slaves attribute superhuman powers to Bras Coupé? Why were they compelled to march past his body?

6. a) Why was High John de Conquer unknown to the white people of his time, and why has he become unknown to the present generation of Negroes? How does the author's comparison of High John to King Arthur relate to this question?

b) What did High John represent in the Negro spirit that enabled it to endure the years of slavery with dignity and courage?

7. a) What characteristics of frontier America did Paul Bunyan personify?
   b) Do you think Bunyan is valid today as a symbol of America?

8. How are Paul Bunyan and Pecos Bill similar? In what ways do they differ?

9. a) Do you think Benét intended William Sycamore to be taken as a real person, or as a symbol? Explain your answer.
   b) Explain the last stanza. To whom is William Sycamore speaking? What is his message? Why do you suppose he expresses such a preference?

ON YOUR OWN

1. If you are interested in the origin of the famous bowie knife, read "The Bowie Knife," in *A Treasury of Southern Folklore,* by B. A. Botkin, pages 334–338.

2. For a fictional treatment of Bras Coupé, read *The Grandissimes,* a novel by George W. Cable.

3. If you would like to read a lively collection of Paul Bunyan tales, read *Paul Bunyan*, by James Stevens.

4. Read the chapter in John Steinbeck's novel *The Red Pony* called "The Leader of the People." How does Grandfather resemble William Sycamore?

V

Tales of the Supernatural

N o matter how civilized man becomes, his interest in the supernatural persists. Tales of witches, ghosts, devils, and "things that go bump in the night" abound in American folklore.

The early settlers were not at all influenced by the supernatural beliefs of the Indians, but brought their own tales from Europe. French-influenced Louisiana had its stories of werewolves, or loups-garous. English tales of witches came to America with the colonists of Massachusetts and elsewhere. One supernatural figure found in the folklore of all Christian countries was the Devil, and as a result, Devil tales quickly spread throughout America.

The West, less influenced by European tradition, did not produce as much occult folklore as the rest of America, or else ghosts and witches did not thrive well in the wide open spaces. As a result, only one of the selections in this chapter comes from the West, and that one is Mexican in origin.

THE DEVIL IN TEXAS

by Jovitá Gonzales

The theme of a clever man outwitting the Devil is a popular one in American folklore. In this lively tale from Texas, Pedro de Urdemañas, an archetypal Latin trickster, thwarts the Devil by sending him to a place worse than Hell itself!

It was an abnormally hot day in Hell. The big devils and the little devils were all busy feeding the fires, making final preparations to give a warm reception to a barber, a student and a banker who had announced their arrival. A timid knock sounded on the door, and Satan, who was sitting on a throne of flames, sent one of his henchmen to see who the arrivals might be. In walked four men. One, razor in hand, gave away his profession; the second held on to a wallet like Judas Iscariot to his; the third exhibited a notebook devoid of notes. The three were abnormally terrified. The fourth did not appear a bit impressed by the fiery reception awarded them, but with the coolness and nonchalance of one accustomed to such things glanced about with a look of curiosity. He was an athletic sort of a man, wore a five-gallon hat, *chivarras* and spurs, and played with a lariat he held in his hands. He seemed to be as much at home at the others were terrified. Before he was assigned any particular work, he walked to where a devil was shoveling coals, and, taking the shovel from his hands, began to work. Satan was so much impressed that he paid no attention to the others but went to where the stranger was. He did not like this man's attitude at all. He liked to watch the agony on the face of the condemned, but here was this man as cool as a September morn. He went through the flames, over the flames, into the flames and did not mind the heat at all. This was more than his Satanic Majesty could endure. Approaching the man, he commanded him to stop and listen to what he had to say. But the man would not stop and kept on working.

"Oh, well," said Satan, "if that's the way you feel keep it up, but I really would like to know something about you and where you come from."

"If that's the case," the stranger replied, "then I must satisfy your curiosity. I am Pedro de Urdemañas by name. I have lived through the ages deceiving people, living at the expense of women who are foolish enough to fall in love with me. Now as a beggar, now as a blind man I have earned my living. As a gypsy and a horse trader in Spain, then as a soldier of fortune in the new world, I have managed to live without working. I have lived through the equatorial heat of South America, through the cold of the Andes and the desert heat of the Southwest. I am immune to the heat and the cold, and really bask in the warmth of this place."

The Devil was more impressed than ever and wanted to know more of this strange personage.

"Where was your home before you came here?" he continued.

"Oh, in the most wonderful land of all. I am sure you would love it. Have you ever been in Texas?"

The devil shook his head.

"Well, that's where I come from. It is a marvelous country."

"Indeed?" said the Evil One, "and what is it like?"

Pedro described the land in such glowing terms that the Devil was getting interested in reality. "And what's more," continued Pedro, "there is plenty of work for you down there."

At this Satan cocked his ears, for if there was one thing he liked better than anything else it was to get more workers for his shops.

"But listen," he confided, "you say there are many cows there. Well, you see I have never seen one and would not know what to do were I to see one."

"You have nothing to fear about that. There is a marked similarity between you and a cow. Both have horns and a tail. I am sure you and the cows will become very good friends."

After this comparison, Satan was more anxious than ever to go to this strange land where cows lived.

So early the next day before the Hell fires were started, he set out earth-bound. Since his most productive work had been done in the cities and he knew nothing of ranch life, Satan left for Texas gaily appareled in the latest New York style. He knew how to dress, and as he strolled through the earth seeking for Texas, he left many broken hearts in his path.

Finally, on an August day he set foot on a little prairie surrounded by thorny brush, near the lower Rio Grande. It was a hot day indeed. The sand that flew in whirlwinds was hotter than the flames of the infernal region. It burned the Devil's face and scorched his throat. His tongue was swollen; his temples throbbed with the force of a hammer beat. As he staggered panting under the noonday heat, he saw something that gladdened his eyes. A muddy stream glided its way lazily across a sandy bed. His eyes caught sight of a small plant bearing red berries, and his heart gladdened at the sight of it. It was too good to be true. Here was what he most wished for— water and fresh berries to eat. He picked a handful of the ripest and freshest, and with the greediness of the starved put them all into his mouth. With a cry like the bellow of a bull he ducked his head in the stream. He was burning up. The fire that he was used to was nothing compared to the fire from chili peppers that now devoured him.

But he went on, more determined than ever to know all about the land that he had come to see. That afternoon he saw something that, had he not been a devil, would have reminded him of heaven. The ripest of purple figs were growing on a plant that was not a fig tree.

"Here," thought Satan, "is something I can eat without any fear. I remember seeing figs like these in the Garden of Eden." Hungrily he reached for one, but at the first bite he threw it away with a cry of pain. His mouth and tongue were full of thorns. With an oath and a groan he turned from the prickly pear and continued his journey.

Late that same day, just before sunset, he heard the barking of dogs. He continued in that direction from whence the sound came, and soon he came to a ranch house. A group of men, dressed like Pedro de Urdemañas—that new arrival in

Hell who had sent him to Texas—ran here and there on horses gesticulating. The sight of them rather cheered Satan up.

And then he saw what Pedro told him he resembled—a cow. Here was a blow indeed. Could he, the king of Hell, look like one of those insipid creatures, devoid of all character and expression? Ah, he would get even with Pedro on his return and send him to the seventh hell, where the greatest sinners were and the fire burnt the hottest. His reflections were interrupted by something that filled him with wonder. One of the mounted men threw a cow down by merely touching its tail. "How marvelous!" thought Satan. "I'll learn the trick so I can have fun with the other devils when I go back home."

He approached one of the *vaqueros* and in the suavest of tones said, "My friend, will you tell me what you did to make the lady cow fall?"

The cowboy looked at the city man in surprise, and with a wink at those around him replied, "Sure, just squeeze its tail."

Satan approached the nearest cow—an old gentle milk cow—gingerly, and squeezed its tail with all his might.

Now, as all of you know, no decent cow will allow any one, even though it be the king of Devils, to take such familiarity with her. She ceased chewing her cud, and, gathering all her strength in her hind legs, shot out a kick that sent Satan whirling through the air.

Very much upset and chagrined, he got up. But what hurt more were the yells of derision that greeted him. Without even looking back, he ran hell-bound, and did not stop until he got home. The first thing he did on his arrival was to expel Pedro from the infernal region. He would have nothing to do with one who had been the cause of his humiliation. And since then Satan has never been in Texas, and Pedro de Urdemañas still wanders through the Texas ranches always in the shape of some fun-loving *vaquero*.

HOW JACK O'LANTERNS CAME TO BE

by Zora Neale Hurston

Once again, the Devil gets his "comeuppance," this time from a powerful Negro named Big Sixteen.

It was slavery time . . . when Big Sixteen was a man. They called 'im Sixteen 'cause dat was de number of de shoe he wore. He was big and strong and Ole Massa looked to him to do everything.

One day Ole Massa said, "Big Sixteen, Ah b'lieve Ah want you to move dem sills Ah had hewed out down in de swamp."

"I yassuh, Massa."

Big Sixteen went down in de swamp and picked up dem 12 × 12's and brought 'em on up to de house and stack 'em. No one man ain't never toted a 12 × 12 befo' nor since.

So Ole Massa said one day, "Go fetch in de mules. Ah want to look 'em over."

Big Sixteen went on down to de pasture and caught dem mules by de bridle but they were contrary and balky and he tore de bridles to pieces pullin' on 'em, so he picked one of 'em up under each arm and brought 'em up to Old Massa.

He says, "Big Sixteen, if you kin tote a pair of balky mules you kin do anything. You kin ketch de Devil."

"Yassuh, Ah kin, if you git me a nine-pound hammer and a pick and shovel!"

Ole Massa got Sixteen de things he ast for and tole 'im to go ahead and bring him de Devil.

Big Sixteen went out in front of de house and went to diggin'. He was diggin' nearly a month befo' he got where he wanted. Then he took his hammer and went and knocked on de Devil's door. Devil answered de door hisself.

"Who dat out dere?"

"It's Big Sixteen."

"What you want?"

"Wanta have a word wid you for a minute."

Soon as de Devil poked his head out de door, Sixteen lammed him over de head wid dat hammer and picked 'im up and carried 'im back to Ole Massa.

Ole Massa looked at de dead Devil and hollered, "Take dat ugly thing 'way from here, quick! Ah didn't think you'd ketch de Devil sho 'nuff."

So Sixteen picked up de Devil and throwed 'im back down de hole.

Way after while, Big Sixteen died and went up to Heben. But Peter looked at him and tole 'im to g'wan 'way from dere. He was too powerful. He might git outa order and there wouldn't be nobody to handle 'im. But he had to go somewhere so he went on to hell.

Soon as he got to de gate de Devil's children was playin' in de yard and they seen 'im and run to de house, says, "Mama, mama! Dat man's out dere dat kilt papa!"

So she called 'im in de house and shet de door. When Sixteen got dere she handed 'im a li'l piece of fire and said, "You ain't comin' in here. Here, take dis hot coal and g'wan off and start you a hell uh yo' own."

So when you see a Jack O'Lantern in de woods at night you know it's Big Sixteen wid his piece of fire lookin' for a place to go.

LOUIE ALEXANDER

by John Bennett

In the old days, fiddling was considered sinful, and fiddlers, especially talented ones, supposedly got their powers by selling their souls to the Devil. This story, as told by Walter Mayrant, is a warning to all would-be fiddlers!

In the old days when the Devil taught the fiddlers we had much better music than we have now.

Jack Calhoun was a fine fiddler; but Louie Alexander was finest of all.

Some say he was taught by Dicky Brux, the great conjure man on the Dorchester Road. Some say the Devil taught him. Old Caesar says he was taught by the Devil, not by Dicky Brux; no man could fiddle like Louie Alexander unless he had been taught by the Devil.

Louie was a Charleston man, short-bodied, heavy and dark. He was a pleasant fellow, friendly with all, jovial and fond of a joke. And he could play the fiddle as if he had been born with a fiddle in his hands. There never has been another fiddler like Louie Alexander. He could play equally well the banjo, guitar or bull fiddle; he could play a lead horn fit to make a man cry. But with his fiddle he could almost conjure your heart out. When white folks heard Louie Alexander play they always said: "The Devil is in that man." They called him "The Black Pickaninny."

One who wants to learn to play from the Devil must take a yellow yam, a hen egg, and a black fowl to the crossroads in the dark of the moon, stake the fowl, break the egg, lay the yam down in the egg, and call the Devil seven times. He will come on the seventh call.

Louie did these things so; then called the Devil. There was the Devil, sitting on a burnt gum stump. "What do you want?" says he.

"To play the fiddle better than any man alive or dead," said Louie. "I will pay whatever you ask."

"That's a fair bargain," said the Devil; and taught Louie how to play the fiddle better than any man alive or dead. "Thank you," said Louie.

"Just keep your thanks," said the Devil. "I will take my own pay."

After that no man could play the fiddle like Louie Alexander. He could play a whole tune on one note; or a whole song on one string; and when he played for dancing everyone that heard him had to dance, . . . they could not keep their feet still.

When Louie played the Devil was in it. The women sang at the top of their voices; and the dancer sang tunes that could only come from the Devil. The women all pushed around him like cows, butting to be next. Louie just scratched their heads with his fiddle bow: women were about as pleasing to him as a houseful of smoke. The men whooped and hopped and jumped. They forgot their troubles, and all their cares; the girls were pretty, drink was free; and everyone might have his fill. They just whooped it up all night. Every minute the party got louder, with buckets of white mule and bottles of beer. The girls pulled their clothes off, and everything was delightful. And nobody who came into the hall ever left it from candle-lighting on Saturday night to sunrise Sunday morning; they forgot how to use the door.

And never once, the whole night long, would Louie ever skip a beat or lose the time; he fiddled like the Devil himself; and the Devil never loses any time. Everbody had a pig's fill till the first dong of the old church bell put an end to the doing.

Louie gave a hot supper every Saturday night. And every Sunday morning, after Louie's hot supper, somebody got carried home, dead.

At the dong of the bell Louie laid down his fiddle; and when he laid down his fiddle the party was over. They all went home. They forgot where they had been, or what they had done, or how they had behaved themselves. All they knew was that they were too tired to go to work; so they went home and slept all day; nobody went where he was hired, or where anybody expected him to be; and nobody cared a damn. The

Devil was in Louie Alexander's music. But Louie laughed, and kept his secret.

After a while he went down to Beaufort and got him a fine string orchestra there. The people in Beaufort and Port Royal welcomed so famous a fiddler, and took the opportunity to have hot suppers and dances. And as it had been in Charleston it was in Port Royal and Beaufort; people hailed Louie Alexander as the greatest of all fiddlers, dead or alive.

But a gift from the Devil is a debt in the end.

Louie lived many years in Beaufort. His house was on the Point, behind Beaufort, a solitary place.

One day the apothecary missed Louie who went every day by the apothecary shop. "What's become of Louie Alexander?" he asked. Nobody knew. So they went to the lonely house on the Point where Louie had lived. When they opened the door there was Louie, dead, in a heap on the bed . . . like the old song says:

> Dere lay Louie stretch' on de bed,
> Shoe on his feet, and hat on his head,
> And a stink like de Debble behine 'im!

Louie lay there on the bed, his eyes wide open, staring and his mouth twisted. His face was gray as an alley cat at night, and there was white froth on his lips. The look on Louie Alexander's face was not that of a sweet and quiet death.

Joe Bythewood said that there had been a light in Louie's house all night. The oil in his lamp was burnt out, the wick was charred to the brass, and the brass was burnt black. The soot from the burnt wick had fallen like snow on everything; Louie's face was covered with it, and the bedding.

Some said he died of poison, from the foam on his lips. But the law couldn't prove it; nobody believed it; and nobody believes it to this day.

The Devil, who had taught him to fiddle, had come for

his pay; and, willy-nilly, ready or not, he just took Louie Alexander's soul and went home. On the table by the bedside were pen, ink and paper, a regular contract paper; and across the back of the paper, in a big, sprawl hand, showing that it had been written by a big man, were the three words:

PAID IN FULL

Nobody could have written that but the Devil.

THE WITCH BRIDLE[1]
by John Harrington Cox

To rural folk in the South, witches were very real and caused no end of trouble, but they could be dealt with by a resourceful, courageous man like Old Braham.

Old Braham lived in a one-room log house close to the Cheat River, somewhere above Albrightsville, Preston County. In one corner of the house was a big old-fashioned open fireplace, and in the opposite corner was his bed.

Once upon a time just about midnight, he awoke from his first dream to hear men talking in his room. He knew that they thought he was asleep, and in order to find out what was going on, he concluded not to let them know that he was awake. By this means he soon found out their errand. He caught every word they said, although they talked in a low voice, and by the dim light that flickered from the charred embers of the fireplace, he saw everything they did out of one corner of his eye.

The intruders were six out of a band of seven witch-men of that community, who kept their witch-bridles and their

[1]The following tale, collected under the auspices of the West Virginia Folklore Society, was taken down from the telling of Miss Sarah Alice Barnes, Bruceton Mills, Preston County, on April 10, 1916. Miss Barnes learned it from hearing it told in the community.—J. H. C.

bowl of magic ointment under old Braham's hearthstone. He inferred from their conversation that any one who could put one of the witch-bridles on an animal or a person was able to turn that animal or person into a horse and subject it entirely to his will. Furthermore, any one who rubbed some of the ointment three times on his forehead between the eyes and also on his throat, and then made a cross three times with it over his heart, could fly like a bird. Old Braham also gathered from the men's talk their business there that evening was to ride off his calves, as they had frequently done before, to a witches' meeting somewhere up on Scraggly Mountain several miles away.

As the seventh witch-man had not come, the other six got ready for their trip without him. They rolled back the big hearthstone and each took one of the bridles for himself and laid it aside. Then they all anointed themselves with the ointment out of the bowl and replaced the hearthstone. Taking up their bridles again, the first witch-man waved his arms and flew up the chimney; another man waved his arms and flew up the chimney; a third waved his arms and flew up the chimney; a fourth waved his arms and flew up the chimney; and the other two did likewise.

Out of the chimney all the witch-men flew, down over the yard and into the calf lot. The head witch-man bridled the big spotted calf and jumped on its back; down the calf lot it went, jumped the fence, and ran down the road. The second man bridled the big red calf and mounted it; down the lot it went, jumped the fence and ran down the road. The third man bridled the big black calf and swung himself upon its back; down the lot it went, jumped the fence and ran down the road. The fourth witch-man bridled the big brown calf and mounted its back; down the lot it went, jumped the fence, and ran down the road. The fifth witch-man bridled up the big roan calf, leaped upon its back, and prodded it with his spur; down the lot it went, jumped the fence, and ran down the road. Not much choice was left for the sixth man, only the little white calf and the little red calf. The white being the prettier, he chose that, bridled it and jumped upon its back; down the lot it went, jumped the fence and ran down the road as the others had done, all bound for Scraggly Mountain.

In the meantime old Braham no longer pretended to be asleep, but had arisen and was making some investigations on his own account. He resolved that he, too, would turn witch, take advantage of his newly acquired knowledge, and ride to Scraggly Mountain that night. The hearthstone was heavy, but he was strong and succeeded in dislodging it. He drew out the remaining witch-bridle, anointed himself with the ointment in the bowl, and replaced the stone. Then as he had seen the witch-men do, he flapped his arms, flew up the chimney, over the yard, and down into the calf lot. He bridled the little red calf, the only one left, and jumped on its back; down the lot it went, jumped the fence, and ran down the road at a death pace, determined to overtake the other calves, all bound for Scraggly Mountain.

So fast the little red calf ran with old Braham on its back, that by the time the others had left the road and run across a piece of fallow land to Nixon's Ford, it was in sight of them. Old Braham watched his other calves with the witch-men on their backs leap the stream. The big spotted calf cleared it with apparent ease. The big red calf, the big black calf, the big brown calf, did the same. The big roan calf, being a little smaller, barely cleared the stream, one of her hind feet coming down in the sand and water. The little white calf made a great bound, jumped nearly across, waded out, and climbed the steep bank on the other side.

By this time old Braham on the little red calf was at the ford. He had seen how the smaller ones of the other calves had barely made the leap across, but his calf, the smallest of all, had certainly out-run all the rest and he determined to make the effort. So he bumped the little red calf in the sides with both the heels of his boots and it made a tremendous spring forward. But the great effort it made caused it to leap sidewise and it came down in the middle of the stream on a fallen tree that served as a foot-log. When the calf with old Braham on its back struck the log, it burst and rolled over into the water. Old Braham managed to hold on to the witch-bridle with one hand and grasp the foot-log with the other. The bridle pulled out of the mouth of the calf, which turned into a red lizard and sank into the stream.

With the bridle still in his hand, old Braham managed to pull himself up on to the fallen tree. But no sooner did he find himself safely anchored on the log, than down from above out of a tree, jumped a big blue cat, right on to his back. Its weight was so heavy that old Braham was considerably stunned when it struck him; and before he had time to realize what had crashed down upon his unprotected back, the cat had seized the witch-bridle, slipped it into his mouth, and mounted him. "Ho!" said the big blue cat. "I'll get to ride to the witch meeting yet. Old man, if you wanted to burst your little red calf so that I could not ride him, well and good. I'll just ride you in his stead. I knew that one of the seven witch-men was not along with the rest. Now for Scraggly Mountain. Ho! come up!"

The cat gave the witch-bridle a big twitch and slapped old Braham smartly on one side of the face with one big blue paw, and then on the other side of the face with the other paw. There was nothing that old Braham could do except to crawl off on his hands and feet as the big blue cat's horse. He scrambled off the log, up the steep stony bank, and climbed the high, tiresome mountain, the big blue cat jumping up and down on his back, jerking the bridle, clucking to him to go faster and striking him with his claws and the end of the bridle rein. When they came near the place where the witches' meeting was to be held, the big blue cat rode his horse up to a tree and tied him so as to be in readiness when the frolic was over and he wanted to ride back.

The revel lasted a long time, but at last the big blue cat returned, very weary. He found old Braham still tied up securely to the tree, just where he had left him. The old cat, being tired and sleepy, concluded to lie down and rest awhile before he rode down the mountain. Accordingly, he stretched himself out under a neighboring tree and went to sleep.

While the big blue cat was asleep, old Braham began to think some on his own account. If he could only get the witch-bridle out of his own mouth and slip it into the cat's! He concluded to try it and after a great effort succeeded in slipping the bit. Then he stepped over stealthily to where the big cat slept. Cautiously he slipped the bit into his mouth, gave the rein a great jerk, and shook him awake. The big blue cat awoke in a fit of temper at such rough treatment and began to growl and strike with his paws.

"Oh, no," said old Braham softly. "I was your horse up the mountain, now I guess you'll be mine down. Turn about is only fair play. Since I carried you up, it is only right that you carry me down. And since it is much easier to carry a load down hill than it is to carry it up, I shall have to ask you to carry me the rest of the way home in order to even up with you."

No amount of pleading on the part of the cat availed, and so they set off down the mountain, the old blue cat carrying old Braham. The old man was heavy and the cat lost all his courage and bravado when he found he was conquered. His paws gave out and began to bleed, so that old Braham had to stop at a blacksmith shop and have him shod. Then they went on again, the old blue cat bending and groaning under his great load.

When old Braham was nearly home, the old blue cat drew up before a dilapidated hut and wanted to turn in there.

Since he carried the old man so well, Braham's heart was considerably eased and his hatred of the cat a great deal lessened. It was not very much farther to his house and he concluded to let the old cat go and walk the rest of the way home. He dismounted, but kept the witch-bridle firmly in the cat's mouth, which, with old Braham at his side, made straight for the door of the hut. As soon as he stepped upon the door sill, he was transformed into an old witch-woman. The old witch had quickly turned on Braham with a smile of triumph on her evil face and said, "Um huh! you see who I am! I am an old witch. I'll bewitch you and you'll die."

"Um huh! and you see who I am," replied old Braham. "I'm your master; I've still got the witch-bridle in your mouth. It's a good plan not to crow until you're out of the woods. I am going to chain you up to that staple in the wall in there, then go home and make a silver bullet, and come back and shoot you."

The old witch lamented and pleaded for her freedom and her life, but old Braham was obstinate. He tied her with a chain to the staple and went home to mould the silver bullet.

Soon after old Braham left, the sun came up and it was full day. Then there came a man to the old witch to plead with her to unwitch his son, "Shonny," whom she had bewitched the evening before. The child was in the first throes of the pains of witchcraft, but as he had been bewitched less than twenty-four hours, the old witch did not as yet suffer any pains, not seeing him. When the man looked in and saw the old witch chained to a staple in the wall, he was at first much gratified. However, she soon began to blarney and to try to make terms of peace with him. In her slyest way she told him she would unwitch "Shonny" and never work any of her spells on his family again if he would release her. In proof of her good faith, she drew a silver ring from the index finger of her left hand and gave it to the man. Thereupon, he went out, but returned in a short time with a sharp stone. With this he cut a link in the chain that bound the old witch and she was free. Then the man departed for home.

No sooner was he gone than the old woman hobbled across to an old wooden cupboard that stood in one corner of the hut. She reached up and from above the cupboard took down a brightly scoured shining tin pan, her witch pan, by means of which she worked her spells. With a leer, she sat down on her door sill in the bright sunshine. The rays that glanced off the bright tin pan were too dazzling for the ordinary eye to behold, but the old witch, whose eyes had been hardened to it by the devil, looked steadily at the bright tin in order to weave her spell. She tapped the pan with her ring finger, saying as she tapped, "One, two, three." Then she began to mutter her incantations: "I, here on this brightly scoured tin pan consecrate myself anew to the devil and put my soul in thralldom to him on condition that old Ebenezer Braham shall die as surely as the sun shall set this evening and rise tomorrow morning, and that he shall be in pain, unendurable pain, henceforth till he die, so help me dev—."

But while the old witch was working her spell on old Braham, old Braham himself was not idle. He had run to make the silver bullet with which to shoot the old witch as he told her he would do. A good deal of time passed before he got his bullet done and put it into his gun. He had also drawn a crude picture of the old witch on a piece of paper. While she was muttering her incantations, old Braham felt the spell coming over him. Quickly seizing his gun and the paper picture, he ran out through the open door, hung the picture on a tree, and running back a short distance, took aim and fired. The silver bullet pierced the heart of the picture of the old witch and sunk into the bark of the tree.

Just as the bullet struck the heart of the picture of the old witch, she was sitting in her doorway over the bright tin pan, saying her last word, "Devil." Suddenly, she clapped her hand to her heart and cried out, "O my God! I'm shot! I'm killed!" and fell back dead.

ESAU AND THE GORBEY

by Gerald Averill

This odd and gruesome tale was widespread in Maine lumber camps. The gorbey is probably a Canada Jay, and it was believed that gorbeys were the souls of dead woodsmen. Anyone harming a gorbey could expect to have the same thing happen to him.

. . . Now, before I relate the story almost exactly as it was told to me, and this I am able to do because I wrote it down at its ending, I must digress a bit. . . . Since this bird is one of the principals in the tale, it is necessary to speak a little of the Canada Jay, or—as it was commonly called by the woodsmen—the gorbey or moose bird.

Years ago, when I first went into the woods north of Moosehead, these birds were very plentiful and very tame and fearless. Lunching alone on the trail, I have had them fly down and take crumbs from my fingers a number of times. Wherever there was food or a campground, there was sure to be a flock of the sooty-gray little thieves hanging around and nobody ever thought of harming them until in later years the sports found them easy targets for their twenty-twos. It was commonly believed among the older men that it was exceedingly bad luck for anyone to offer them harm or to drive them away, in spite of the fact that I have seen them around wangans and open camps so thick that they became a real nuisance. Margarine especially attracted them, and many times I have seen them swoop down and scoop a beakful from right under the noses of a feeding crew seated at an outdoor table. Sometimes when a man was recovering from a big drunk and hanging on the edge of the D.T.'s, this could be very disconcerting, but the ordinary run of oldtimers took it as a matter of course. The gorbeys are not nearly as numerous these days, and it has been a long while since I have seen one.

Rocky Emmons told [me] the story fully, and this is the way of it:

"In the old days, an' I will not say how long gone it was, Esau was a bold giant of a man. He took charge in the camps an' on the drives, an' a hard man he was on a crew. His temper was quick an' his hand heavy an' he would take no lip from no man great or small. He had a thick head of yeller hair an' a great silky beard of the same, an' he spent hours combin' both the beard and his head till they would glisten an' gleam like yeller gold. There was a great mat of hair upon his chest an' it was thick, too, upon his arms and legs, an' he was sin-fully proud of it all. This hair was a sign to him of his strength an' manhood an', bein' who an' what he was, no man made light of it twice. He was a cruel man with the might of an ox an' the heart of a weasel. No man called him 'friend,' but he could drive a crew an' get out the timber.

" 'Twas in a camp on the north side of Pogy Mountain on a day in January that the thing happened—a day of bitter cold an' drivin' snow, dry ice that could peel the hide from a man's face. Esau was wild because the crew laid in an' he spent the day goddamning them all for a bunch of old women, even though he knew no man, exceptin' perhaps himself, could live an' work outside the way it was. After the noon meal, he calmed down some and sat in a great chair he had made for himself an' began to comb his hair an' beard. Most of the men was tired an' napped, but Jean Ayette from across the line, meself an' two others got out a deck of cards, but it was too cold to play. The wind shrieked an' howled over an' around the roof, drivin' the dry snow in through the chinkin', an' every once in a while you could hear one of the cedar roof shakes loosen up and clatter. Half the time the stove wouldn't draw an' would puke great puffs of smoke an' ashes out into the room. It was one cruel, God-awful day, boy, the like of which I have never seen since.

"It must have been around two o'clock when the storm was at its worst that the bird come—the little half-froze gorbey. He come an' fluttered his wings ag'inst the winder an' the wind caught him an' blew him away like a wisp of paper. An' then in the space of a few breaths he was back ag'in, an' Esau looked up an' seen him there flutterin' an' beatin' his wings ag'inst the pane. The bird dropped to the sill an' huddled into the corner where the frame was let into the logs, an' Esau got onto his feet an' stepped quick as a cat to the winder.

"He pulled the pegs that held in the frame an' scooped up the bird in his fist, yellin' for one of us to put the winder back in. Jean an' me put it back an' Esau sat down by the stove. The little gray head, lookin' this way an' that, peeked up through his fist an' the comical black-rimmed beady eyes never so much as blinked. He held the bird up level with his eyes an' talked soft an' easy to it.

" 'Ha,' he says, 'ye have a familiar look about ye, me little gray crow. Ye look like Frenchy Aucoin with them two black eyes I gave him over on Black Brook two years gone, but Frenchy slipped on a jam an' went to hell.'

"He held the bird up closer an' looked an' looked, an' the bird looked back.

" 'Now,' Esau went on, 'they's some that believe men has souls an' when they die, the souls come back an' flitter around. You wouldn't be the little thievin' soul of Frenchy Aucoin, would ye, now?'

"The bird turned his head this way and that an' then he

pulled back his little neck an' gave a tiny peck at the hand that held him.

" 'Well now,' croons Esau, soft an' easy, 'well now, will ye look at that! I take him in an' warm him in me own soft hands an' he bites me. Right before me own crew in me own camp the little gray crumb of a thievin' bastard of a crow bites me! Well, me fine rooster, if ye don't like it here, back ye go outside where ye belong. But first, before ye become over-heated, leave us take off a few clothes.'

"An' then, whilst the whole caboodle of us stood by in shame an' fear, he opened his fist, spread an' clamped fast a wing with his thumb an' held the other open with a finger and, quick an' dainty as you please, he began to pluck the soft, short breast an' body feathers. The camp was deathly still, barrin' the howlin' o' the wind an' we could all hear the small rip-rip as the feathers came free. The gorbey squeaked once, an' then ag'in, an' was quiet.

" 'Twas but a minute he worked, for he was quick with his hands, an' then he let out a beller of laughter an' held up the bird by the tips of his two wings. Ah, me lad, 'twas a pitful sight, all the feathers stripped clean from the body an' only the wing an' tail feathers left. Even the neck he had picked, but the little black eyes were bright an' glittern' an', whilst we looked, the head turned an' dipped an' the small beak plucked at his fingers.

" 'An' now,' said Esau, an' there was the very devil in the tone of his voice, 'an' now, me little naked chicken, nobody asked ye here. Ye have been warmed an' entertained an' be damned to ye. Should ye turn out to be the black-eyed soul of Mister Aucoin, ye'll flutter back to hell an' be warm enough. An' if ye should be jest the little thievin' jay bird I think ye are, then ye'll freeze quick an' easy, so out ye go.'

"He folded the bird's wings close to its body, closed his fist around it, an' steppin' to the winder, he loosed the sash an' thrust forth the naked bird into the storm. It turned once an' spread itself ag'inst the glass like one crucified, an' then the wind whisked it away."

The old teamster paused for refreshment. His voice had taken on a slight burr, and his suspicion of a brogue was growing by the minute.

"There was little sleep amongst us that night," he went on. "We ate an' stretched on our bunks. Them was the days when we slept ten or a dozen under one long spread, an' when one turned in the night, all must do the same. The storm grew worse toward dark an' it tore at the camp until we thought surely the roof would leave her. Along towards mornin' the wind died an' we dozed off an' woke again when the bull-cook stoked the stove and lit the lanterns. I was half asleep when he rolled us out an' was rubbin' the sleep from me eyes an' gropin' for me stags, when I heard the noise—a queer sound it was, a kind of a cross between a bleat an' a groan. It came from over in the corner where the wooden sink an' the water barrel stood, but before I could turn meself for a look, there was a gabble of French an' I seen Ayette down on his knees crossin' hisself whilst others of the crew stood starin' an' stiff with fear.

" 'Twas Esau's habit—to toughen him, as he said—to strip naked in the morn an' splash the icy water over his head an' chest, an' there he stood in the corner by the sink, white an' naked an', by the Little Old White-Eyed an' the Holy Old Mackinaw, there was no wisp of hair upon him at any place! The thick mane of hair, the glossy beard, his brows an' even his eye-winkers was gone. The hair from his body was gone, too, an' he stood, scared an' shiverin', as white an' smooth as one of them marble statues of a man.

"The place was like a madhouse. The Frenchman Ayette was half mad with fear, an' Neil Hart, a Black Irishman with a tongue as sharp as a new file, cursed Esau, the mother that bore him, the man that fathered him and that man's father before him. Up an' down an' over an' under an' before an' behind he cursed Esau, until the Irishman's eyes rolled in his head, the froth came from his mouth, an' we could no longer understand his gibberish. An' Esau did nothin' but stand there in his nakedness an' tremble, an' it come to us that with his hair the best or the worst of him was gone with it, an' after a time we covered his shame with his clothes, hung his turkey on his shoulders an' druv him out from among us with kicks an' blows.

"The storm had stopped an' he went flounderin' off down the mountain through the deep snow. No man knows where he went, but for a matter of two years he was seen by none of us. 'Twas agreed that we would not speak of the thing, but the Frenchman Ayette could not hold his tongue an' Hart had a loose mouth while in his cups. The tale went round, but 'twas told so many different ways an' so wildly that there seemed no truth to it at all, an' as those that were there at the camp on Pogy were killed off or died in their beds, the truth of the matter was lost entirely.

"They say that the Big Feller heard the tale an', believin' in neither good luck nor bad, put Esau on the office payroll as a hunter of stray horses, an' when ye see him now, he is at that work. He travels when an' where he pleases, an' he tells me sunthin' drives him from place to place. There is no rest anywheres for him, for men refuse to sit at table with him or sleep under the same roof. He comes an' goes, an' if ye make note of it, ye'll see that the storms come with him. As for me I can take no harm from him, for no worse luck can come upon me than I have already borne."

THE WRAITH IN THE STORM
by Samuel Adams Drake

In this eerie tale, an old woman receives dreadful news from the supernatural world. Or was it just her imagination?

The number of persons who have testified to having seen the apparitions or death wraiths of dying or deceased friends is already large, as the records of various societies for psychical research bear witness. These phenomena are not in their nature forewarnings of something that is about to happen, but announcements of something that already has happened. They therefore can have no relation to what was formerly known as "second sight."

In spite of all that our much-boasted civilization has done in the way of freeing poor, fallible man from the thraldom of superstition, there is indubitable evidence that a great many people still put faith in direct revelations from the land of spirits. In the course of a quiet chat one evening, where the subject was under discussion, one of the company who had listened attentively, though silently all the while, to all manner of theories, spiced with ridicule, abruptly asked how we would account for the following incident which he went on to relate, and I have set down word for word:—

"My grandparents," he began, "had a son whom they thought all the world of. From all accounts I guess Tom was about one of the likeliest young fellows that could be scared up in a day's journey. Everybody said Tom was bound to make his mark in the world, and at the time I speak of he seemed in a fair way of doing it, too, for at one and twenty he was first mate of the old *Argonaut* which had just sailed for Calcutta. This would make her tenth voyage. Well, as I am telling you, the very day after the *Argonaut* went to sea, a tremendous gale set in from the eastward. It blew great guns. Actually, now, it seemed as if that gale would never stop blowing.

"As day after day went by, and the storm raged on without intermission, you may judge if the hearts of those who had friends at sea in that ship did not sink down and down with the passing hours. Of course, the old folks could think of nothing else.

"Let me see; it was a good bit ago. Ah, yes; it was on the third or four night of the gale, I don't rightly remember which, and it don't matter much, that grandfather and grandmother were sitting together, as usual, in the old family sitting room, he poring over the family Bible as he was wont to do in such cases, she knitting and rocking, or pretending to knit, but both full of the one ever present thought, which each was trying so hard to hide from the other.

"Dismally splashed the raindrops against the window-panes, mournfully the wind whined in the chimney top, while every now and then the fire would spit and sputter angrily on the hearth, or flare up fitfully when some big gust came roaring down the chimney to fan the embers into a fiercer flame. Then there would be a lull, during which, like an echo of the tempest, the dull and distant booming of the sea was borne to the affrighted listener's ears. But nothing I could say would begin to give you an idea of the great gale of 1817.

"Well, the old folks sat there as stiff as two statues, listening to every sound. When a big gust tore over the house and shook it till it rocked again, gran'ther would steal a look at grandmother over his specs, but say never a word. The old lady would give a start, let her hands fall idly upon her lap, sit for a moment as if dazed, and then go on with her knitting again as if her very life depended on it.

"Unable at length to control her feelings, grandmother got up out of her chair, with her work in her hand, went to the window, put aside the curtain, and looked out. I say looked out, for of course all was so pitchdark outside that nothing could be seen, yet there she stood with her white face pressed close to the wet panes, peering out into the night, as if questioning the storm itself of the absent one.

"All at once she drew back from the window with a low cry, saying in a broken voice: 'My God, father, it's Tom in his coffin! They're bringing him up here, to the house.' Then she covered her face with her hands, to shut out the horrid sight.

" 'Set down 'Mandy!' sternly commanded the startled old man. 'Don't be making a fool of yourself. Don't ye know tain't no sech a thing what you're sayin'? Set down, I say, this minnit!'

"But no one could ever convince grandmother that she had not actually seen, with her own eyes, her dear boy Tom, the idol of her heart, lying cold in death. To her indeed it was a revelation from the tomb, for the ship in which Tom had sailed was never heard from."

THE WITCH OF COÖS

by Robert Frost

The attitude of the narrator in this ghost tale is interesting: he neither accepts nor rejects the tale. As he puts it, "They did all the talking."

I stayed the night for shelter at a farm
Behind the mountain, with a mother and son,
Two old-believers. They did all the talking.

MOTHER. Folks think a witch who has familiar spirits
She could call up to pass a winter evening
But won't, should be burned at the stake or something.

Summoning spirits isn't "Button, button,
Who's got the button," I would have them know.

SON. Mother can make a common table rear
And kick with two legs like an army mule.

MOTHER. And when I've done it, what good have I done?
Rather than tip a table for you, let me
Tell you what Ralle the Sioux Control once told me.
He said the dead had souls, but when I asked him
How could that be—I thought the dead were souls,
He broke my trance. Don't that make you suspicious
That there's something the dead are keeping back?
Yes, there's something the dead are keeping back.

SON. You wouldn't want to tell him what we have
Up attic, mother?

MOTHER. Bones—a skeleton.

SON. But the headboard of mother's bed is pushed
Against the attic door: the door is nailed.
It's harmless. Mother hears it in the night
Halting perplexed behind the barrier
Of door and headboard. Where it wants to get
Is back into the cellar where it came from.

MOTHER. We'll never let them, will we, son! We'll never!

SON. It left the cellar forty years ago
And carried itself like a pile of dishes
Up one flight from the cellar to the kitchen,
Another from the kitchen to the bedroom,
Another from the bedroom to the attic,
Right past both father and mother, and neither stopped it.

Father had gone upstairs; mother was downstairs.
I was a baby: I don't know where I was.

MOTHER. The only fault my husband found with me—
I went to sleep before I went to bed,
Especially in winter when the bed
Might just as well be ice and the clothes snow.
The night the bones came up the cellar-stairs
Toffile had gone to bed alone and left me,
But left an open door to cool the room off
So as to sort of turn me out of it.
I was just coming to myself enough
To wonder where the cold was coming from,
When I heard Toffile upstairs in the bedroom
And thought I heard him downstairs in the cellar.
The board we had laid down to walk dry-shod on
When there was water in the cellar in spring
Struck the hard cellar bottom. And then someone
Began the stairs, two footsteps for each step,
The way a man with one leg and a crutch,
Or a little child, comes up. It wasn't Toffile:
It wasn't anyone who could be there.
The bulkhead double-doors were double-locked
And swollen tight and buried under snow.
The cellar windows were banked up with sawdust
And swollen tight and buried under snow.
It was the bones. I knew them—and good reason.
My first impulse was to get to the knob
And hold the door. But the bones didn't try
The door; they halted helpless on the landing,
Waiting for things to happen in their favor.
The faintest restless rustling ran all through them.
I never could have done the thing I did
If the wish hadn't been too strong in me
To see how they were mounted for this walk.

I had a vision of them put together
Not like a man, but like a chandelier.
So suddenly I flung the door wide on him.
A moment he stood balancing with emotion,
And all but lost himself. (A tongue of fire
Flashed out and licked along his upper teeth.
Smoke rolled inside the sockets of his eyes.)
Then he came at me with one hand outstretched,
The way he did in life once; but this time
I struck the hand off brittle on the floor,
And fell back from him on the floor myself.
The finger-pieces slid in all directions.
(Where did I see one of those pieces lately?
Hand me my button-box—it must be there.)
I sat up on the floor and shouted, "Toffile,
It's coming up to you." It had its choice
Of the door to the cellar or the hall.
It took the hall for the novelty,
And set off briskly for so slow a thing,
Still going every which way in the joints, though,
So that it looked like lightning or a scribble,
From the slap I had just now given its hand.
I listened till it almost climbed the stairs
From the hall to the only finished bedroom,
Before I got up to do anything;
Then ran and shouted, "Shut the bedroom door,
Toffile, for my sake!" "Company?" he said,
"Don't make me get up; I'm too warm in bed."
So lying forward weakly on the handrail
I pushed myself upstairs, and in the light
(The kitchen had been dark) I had to own
I could see nothing. "Toffile, I don't see it.
It's with us in the room though. It's the bones."
"What bones?" "The cellar bones—out of the grave."
That made him throw his bare legs out of bed

And sit up by me and take hold of me.
I wanted to put out the light and see
If I could see it, or else mow the room,
With our arms at the level of our knees,
And bring the chalk-pile down. "I'll tell you what—
It's looking for another door to try.
The uncommonly deep snow has made him think
Of his old song, *The Wild Colonial Boy,*
He always used to sing along the tote-road.
He's after an open door to get out-doors.
Let's trap him with an open door up attic."
Toffile agreed to that, and sure enough,
Almost the moment he was given an opening,
The steps began to climb the attic stairs.
I heard them. Toffile didn't seem to hear them.
"Quick!" I slammed to the door and held the knob.
"Toffile, get nails." I made him nail the door shut,
And push the headboard of the bed against it.
Then we asked was there anything
Up attic that we'd ever want again.
The attic was less to us than the cellar.
If the bones liked the attic, let them have it.
Let them stay in the attic. When they sometimes
Come down the stairs at night and stand perplexed
Behind the door and headboard of the bed,
Brushing their chalky skull with chalky fingers,
With sounds like the dry rattling of a shutter,
That's what I sit up in the dark to say—
To no one any more since Toffile died.
Let them stay in the attic since they went there.
I promised Toffile to be cruel to them
For helping them be cruel once to him.

SON. We think they had a grave down in the cellar.

MOTHER. We know they had a grave down in the cellar.

SON. We never could find out whose bones they were.

MOTHER. Yes, we could too, son. Tell the truth for once.
They were a man's his father killed for me.
I mean a man he killed instead of me.
The least I could do was to help dig their grave.
We were about it one night in the cellar.
Son knows the story: but 'twas not for him
To tell the truth, suppose the time had come.
Son looks surprised to see me end a lie
We'd kept all these years between ourselves
So as to have it ready for outsiders.
But tonight I don't care enough to lie—
I don't remember why I ever cared.
Toffile, if he were here, I don't believe
Could tell you why he ever cared himself . . .

She hadn't found the finger-bone she wanted
Among the buttons poured out in her lap.
I verified the name next morning: Toffile.
The rural letter-box said Toffile Lajway.

V. Tales of the Supernatural

TALKING IT OVER

1. In "How Jack O'Lanterns Came to Be" and "The Devil in
   Texas" human beings triumph over the Devil. Compare the
   methods used by Pedro de Urdemañas and Big Sixteen in
   defeating this formidable adversary.

2. a) Why are the witch's last words in "The Witch Bridle" ironic?
b) What attitudes toward witchcraft are revealed in this story, both in the way it is narrated and in the behavior of old Braham?

3. a) In "Esau and the Gorbey," what was Esau's crime, for which he was so severely punished? Was his punishment appropriate?
b) Explain the following statement by the narrator: ". . . it came to us that with his hair the best or the worst of him was gone with it."

4. a) Although "The Witch of Coös" is a ghost story, it contains several touches of humor. Locate and discuss them. Do they have any effect on the story?
b) Explain the lines, "I promised Toffile to be cruel to them/ For helping them be cruel once to him."
c) Is there any evidence in this story that anyone other than the old woman ever saw the bones?
d) Keeping in mind your answers to the previous two questions, how do you think a psychologist might interpret this tale?

ON YOUR OWN

1. The theme of man defeating the Devil is a common one in oral and written literature. Some popular examples are "The Farmer's Curst Wife," an anonymous folk ballad, "The Devil and Daniel Webster," by Stephen Vincent Benét, and *Damn Yankees*, a musical play and movie.

2. An even more common theme is that of a man losing his soul to the Devil in return for worldly success, as in "Louie Alexander." Well-known works dealing with this theme are *Dr. Faustus*, a play by Christopher Marlowe, and "The Devil and Tom Walker," a short story by Washington Irving.

3. Compare "Esau and the Gorbey" to "The Rime of the Ancient Mariner," by Samuel Taylor Coleridge. Consider especially the characters of the protagonists, their crimes, and their punishments.

4. Recent studies in parapsychology have brought to light many stories similar to "The Wraith in the Storm," in which a loved one, although physically many miles away, "appears" to a close friend or relative. Later, it is learned that the loved one died at the exact moment of his supernatural "appearance." Locate other stories of this type and tell the class about them.

VI

America Sings

No study of American folklore would be complete without a selection of folk songs. From Indian times to the present, singing and dancing have been vital to the people of this country. Every Appalachian hamlet and frontier mining camp had its bards, most of whom have long since been forgotten. But their songs have survived, for a long time in oral tradition and more recently on record albums and in folk song concerts. You may have already heard many of the songs included here, without knowing much about their origins. Study the words a little more closely now. They reveal the joys and heartbreaks of lumberjacks, gunmen, railroad workers, slaves, and pioneers—in short, everyone who played a part in the building of America.

THE FROZEN LOGGER

by James Stevens

This humorous ballad was actually composed for a 1929 radio program of Paul Bunyan sketches.[1] Nevertheless, it has been added to the repertoires of many folk singers, most of whom are probably unaware of its synthetic origin.

"I see you are a logger and not a common bum,
  For no one but a logger stirs his coffee with his thumb.

[1]Words and music by James Stevens, TRO © 1951, Folkways Music Publishers, Inc., New York, N.Y. Used by permission.

"My lover was a logger. There's none like him to-day.
  If you'd sprinkle whisky on it, he'd eat a bale of hay.

"He never shaved the whiskers from off his horny side;
  But he'd pound them in with a hammer, then bite 'em off inside.

"My logger came to see me, one freezing winter day.
  He held me in a fond embrace that broke three vertebrae.

"He kissed me when we parted—so hard he broke my jaw,
  And I could not speak to tell him he'd forgot his mackinaw.

"I watched my logger lover going through the snow,
  A-sa'ntering gaily homeward at forty-eight below.

"The weather tried to freeze him. It tried its level best.
  At a hundred degrees below zero, he buttoned up his vest.

"It froze clean down to China. It froze to the stars above.
  At one thousand degrees below zero, it froze my logger love.

"They tried in vain to thaw him. Then, if you'll believe me, sir,
  They made him into ax blades to chop the Douglas fir.

"That's how I lost my lover. And in this cafe I come
  And here I wait till some one stirs his coffee with his thumb.

"And then I tell my story of my love they could not thaw,
  Who kissed me when we parted—so hard he broke my jaw."

THE MILLER'S THREE SONS

*This ballad probably originated in eighteenth-century Eng-
land, but it has achieved wide popularity in this country, par-*

*ticularly in New England and the Appalachian Mountains.
This version is from* The Green Mountain Songster, *collected
transcribed, and edited by Helen Hartness Flanders and others.*

There was a miller who lived in shire,
He had three sons as you shall hear.
He had a mind to make his will
All for to give away his mill.

Chorus:
Sing tra la la day,
Sing tra la la day,
Sing tra le la le day.

The old man called his oldest son,
Saying, "My son, my glass is run,
And if to you my will I'll make,
Come tell me how much toll you'll take."

"Father, O father my name is Dick,
From every bushel I'll take one peck,
From every bushel that I grind,
That I may a good living find."

"You are a fool," the old man said,
"You have not learned the miller's trade.
The mill to you I'll never give,
For by such toll no man can live."

The old man called his second son,
Saying, "My son, my glass is run,
And if to you my will I'll make,
Come tell me how much toll you'll take."

"Father, O father, my name is Ralph,
From every bushel I'll take one half,

From every bushel that I grind,
That I may a good living find."

"You are a fool," the old man said,
"You have not learned the miller's trade.
My mill to you I'll never give,
For by such toll no man can live."

The old man called his youngest son.
Saying, "My son, my glass is run,
And if to you my will I'll make,
Come tell me how much toll you'll take."

"Father, O father I'm your bonnie boy,
And stealing corn is all my joy,
And if I should a living lack,
I'll take the whole and steal the sack."

"The mill is yours," the old man said,
"You have learned the miller's trade.
The mill is yours," the old man cried.
And closed his sinful eyes and died.

CASEY JONES

by Wallace Saunders

Casey Jones, the most famous of all railroad engineers, was born John Luther Jones in Cayce, Missouri, on March 14, 1864. His reckless manner and distinctive whistle made him well-known among the country Negroes along his route. When he died in a spectacular wreck at the age of 26, Wallace Saunders, a Negro railroad worker and folk poet, composed the first version of this ballad. This variant, as good as any, is from Tales of Southern Illinois, *by Charles Neely.*

Come all you rounders, I want you to hear
The story of a brave engineer;
Casey Jones was the rounder's name,
On a big eight-wheeler of a mighty fame.

CHORUS:
Casey Jones, he pushed on the throttle,
Casey Jones was a brave engineer,
Come on, Casey, and blow the whistle,
Blow the whistle so they all can hear.

Now Casey said, "Before I die
There's one more train that I want to try,
And I will try ere many a day
The Union Pacific and the Santa Fe."

Caller called Casey about half past four,
He kissed his wife at the station door,
Climbed in his cab and was on his way,
"I've got my chance on the Santa Fe."

Down the slope he went on the fly,
Heard the fireman say, "You've got a white eye."
Well, the switchman knew by the engine's moan
That the man at the throttle was Casey Jones.

The rain was a-pounding down like lead,
The railroad track was a river bed,
They slowed her down to a thirty-mile gait,
And the south-bound mail was eight hours late.

Fireman says, "Casey, you're running too fast,
You run the black board the last station you passed."
Casey says, "I believe we'll make it through,
For the steam's much better than I ever knew."

Around the curve comes a passenger train,
Her headlight was shining in his eyes through the rain,
Casey blew the whistle a mighty blast
But the locomotive was a-comin' fast.

The locomotives met in the middle of the hill,
In a head-on tangle that's bound to kill,
He tried to do his duty, the yard men said,
But Casey Jones was scalded dead.

Headaches and heartaches and all kinds of pain
They all ride along with the railroad train,
Stories of brave men, noble and grand,
Belong to the life of the railroad man.

SIM WEBB'S ACCOUNT OF THE WRECK

by Eldon Roark

*Sim Webb, a Negro, was Casey Jones's fireman on his fateful
last ride. This account is from an interview with him in 1936,
for* Railroad Magazine.

"We were called in Memphis at 10 P.M. That was Sunday, April 29, 1900. Number 1 was reported to be thirty
minutes late. We had doubled over on Mr. Sam Tate's run on
No. 3 and No. 2, on account of Mr. Tate being ill, and had
come into Memphis that morning at 6:25. But that gave us
time to have a good rest and get ready for our regular run;
and we were both feeling good when we answered the call that
night. We reported at the McLemore Avenue roundhouse and
found old 382 hot and ready to go. We looked her over to see
we had tools, plenty of oil, and everything.

"The regular time for us to leave Poplar Street depot, the main station in those days, was 11:35 P.M. Thirty minutes late would have put us out at twelve five. But it finally happened that No. 1 was an hour and thirty minutes late. Well, we got going. We ran down the track along the Beale Street trestle and on to the Central Station, where we had to stop five minutes. We held a late order saying that we were running thirty minutes late from Memphis to Sardis. There was a freight train coming north, and that was the only thing in front of us.

"We'd been having rainy, foggy weather for two weeks. That night the clouds were mighty dark and low. But Mr. Casey seemed to be in an extra good mood. As we pulled out of Central Station he opened her up and said: "We're going to have a pretty tough time getting into Canton on the dot, but I believe we can do it, barring accidents.' And I replied: 'You can depend on me, Mr. Casey, I'll sure keep her hot.'

"Sardis was our first stop. That's about fifty miles. It took us one hour and two minutes from Poplar Street Station in Memphis to Sardis, which included the stop at Central Station, Memphis. Our actual running time was between forty-five and forty-seven minutes. On south we roared, with everything working just fine. At some places we got to clipping a mile off every fifty seconds. Old 382 was steaming mighty well that night—and using very little fuel. I hadn't even taken down the top coal gate on the tender.

"We made Grenada, fifty miles from Sardis, in what seemed like no time at all. Then came Winona, twenty-three miles further on, and the next stop, Durant, thirty-three miles from Winona. Everything was still going fine. We were whittling that lost time away to nothing, and Mr. Casey was still in high spirits. As we left Durant, he stood up and hollered to me over the boiler head: 'Oh, Sim! The old girl's got her high-heeled slippers on tonight! We ought to pass Way on time.'

"Way was just six miles north of Canton, and he had it

figured out that we'd be back on time when we hit there, and we would coast on it. We hadn't received any more orders. Down the track we went, approaching Vaughan, which is twelve miles above Canton. Vaughan was at the lower end of a double S curve. The north switch was just about the middle of the first S, and as we roared down on it we saw two big red lights. They appeared to me as big as houses. I knew it was a train not in the clear. I could see the lights, but Mr. Casey couldn't, because there was a deep curve to the fireman's side. I yelled to Mr. Casey: 'Look out! We're gonna hit something!'

" 'Jump, Sim!' he shouted, and these were his last words. He was sitting down at the time. I heard him kick the seat out from under him and apply the brakes. About that time I swung down as low off the engine as I could, and hit the dirt. When I came to, half an hour later, Mr. Casey was dead. Our engine had plowed through the caboose of the freight and two other cars—a car of shelled corn and a car of hay!"

THE JAM ON GERRY'S ROCK

The life of a lumberjack was romantic and exciting, but it was, and still is, a dangerous way to make a living, as this ballad proves. "The Jam on Gerry's Rock" probably originated in Michigan, but versions of it quickly spread to logging camps all over the United States. This is the version given by Harold P. Beck in Folklore of Maine.

Now come all of you bold shanty boys, and list while I relate,
Concerning a young riverman and his untimely fate,
Concerning a bold shanty boy, so manly, true and brave,
'Twas on the jam on Gerry's Rock he met a watery grave.

It was on a Sunday morning, as you will quickly hear,
The logs had piled up mountain high, they could not keep them
  clear.
The foreman says, "Turn out, brave boys, with hearts devoid
  of fear,
And we'll break the jam on Gerry's Rock and for English
  Town we'll steer."

Now some of them were willing, while others they were not.
To work on jams on Sundays, they did not think we ought.
But six of those bold shanty boys did volunteer to go,
And break the jam on Gerry's Rock with the foreman Young
  Monroe.

They had not rolled off many logs when they heard his clear
  voice say,
"I'd have you boys be on your guard; this jam will soon give
  way."
Those words were scarely spoken, when the mass did break
  and go,
And it carried off those six brave youths, with their foreman
  Young Monroe.

When the rest of our bold shanty boys the sad news came to
  hear,
In search of those brave comrades to the river they did steer.
Some of their mangled bodies floating down did go,
But crushed and bleeding near the bank was that of Young
  Monroe.

They took him from his watery grave, brushed back his raven
  hair.
There was a fair form among them whose sad cries rent the
  air.

There was a fair girl among them, a maid from Saginaw
Town,
Whose moans and cries rose to the skies for her true love who
had gone down.

Fair Clara was a noble girl, the riverman's true friend.
She, with her widowed mother dear, lived at the river's bend.
The wages of her own true love were brought to her straight
way.
The shanty boys for her made up a generous purse next day.

Now Clara did not long survive. Her heart broke by her grief,
For scarely two months afterwards death came to her release,
And when the time had passed away that she was called to go,
Her last request was granted: to be buried by Young Monroe.

Come all you bold rivermen, I'd have you come and see
Those green mounds by the river side, where grows a hemlock
tree.
The shanty boys cleared off the wood where the lovers there
laid low,
The handsome Clara Vernon and her true love Jack Monroe.

JOHN HENRY

*The setting of this ballad was probably the Big Bend Tunnel
on the C.&O. Railroad around 1870. The hero, John Henry,
was reputedly six feet tall, 200 pounds, and "of pure African
blood." It is believed that his historical death occurred not
after his epic contest with the steam drill, but later in a mountain cave-in. Folk tradition, as in "The Birth of John Henry,"*

which follows, transformed him into a herculean superhero.
As with many folk songs, there are many stanzas and many
variations of the ballad of John Henry.

Well, ev'ry Monday mornin',
When the jaybirds begin to sing,
You can hear dose hammers a mile or more,
You can hear John Henry's hammer ring, Oh Lawdy!
Hear John Henry's hammer ring.

John Henry told his old woman,
"Will you fix my taters soon?
Got ninety miles o' track I've got to line,
Got to line it by de light of de moon, Oh, Lawdy!
Line it by de light o' de moon."

John Henry had a little boy child,
He could hold him in his hand;
Well, the last word I heard that baby say,
"My daddy is a steel-drivin' man, Oh, Lawdy!
Daddy is a steel-drivin' man."

John Henry told his old captain,
Said, "A man ain't nothin' but a man;
An before I'll let your steam drill beat me down
I'll die with dis hammer in my hand, Oh, Lawdy!
Yes, I'll die with dis hammer in my hand."

John Henry told his captain,
"Next time you go to town
Jes' bring me back a twelve pound hammer
For to beat your steel-drivin' down, Oh, Lawdy!
Beat your steel-drivin' down."

John Henry had a old woman,
And her name was Polly Ann.
John Henry tuck sick and dey put him to bed;
Pauline drove steel like a man, Oh, Lawdy!
'Line drove steel like a man.

John Henry had a old woman,
And the dress she wo' was red.
Well, she started down de track never lookin' back,
"Goin' where my man fell dead, Oh, Lawdy!
Where my man fell dead."

Then they taken John Henry to the graveyard,
And they buried him in the sand.
And ev'ry locomotive come a roarin' by
Says, "Dere lies a steel-drivin' man, Oh, Lawdy!
Yes, dere lies a steel-drivin' man.

Well, some said-uh he's from Texas,
And some said he's from Spain;
But I don't give a hoot where dat poor boy was born,
He was a leader of de steel-drivin' gang, Oh, Lawdy!
Leader of de steel-drivin' gang.

THE BIRTH OF JOHN HENRY

by Roark Bradford

Now John Henry was a man, but he's long dead.

The night John Henry was born the moon was copper-colored and the sky was black. The stars wouldn't shine and the rain fell hard. Forked lightning cleaved the air and the earth trembled like a leaf. The panthers squalled in the brake like a baby and the Mississippi River ran upstream a thousand miles. John Henry weighed forty-four pounds.

John Henry was born on the banks of the Black River, where all good rousterbouts come from. He came into the world with a cotton-hook for a right hand and a river song on his tongue:

> "Looked up and down de river,
>   Twice as far as I could see.
> Seed befo' I gits to be twenty-one,
>   De Anchor Line gonter b'long to me, Lawd, Lawd,
>   Anchor Line gonter b'long to me."

They didn't know what to make of John Henry when he was born. They looked at him and then went and looked at the river.

"He got a bass voice like a preacher," his mamma said.

"He got shoulders like a cotton-rollin' rousterbout," his papa said.

"He got blue gums like a conjure man," the nurse woman said.

"I might preach some," said John Henry, "but I ain't gonter be no preacher. I might roll cotton on de boats, but I ain't gonter be no cotton-rollin' rousterbout. I might got blue gums like a conjure man, but I ain't gonter git familiar wid de sperits. 'Cause my name is John Henry, and when fo'ks call me by my name, dey'll know I'm a natchal man."

"His name is John Henry," said his mamma. "Hit's a fack."

"And when you calls him by his name," said his papa, "he's a natchal man."

So about that time John Henry raised up and stretched. "Well," he said, "ain't hit about supper-time?"

"Sho hit's about supper-time," said his mamma.

"And after," said his papa.

"And long after," said the nurse woman.

"Well," said John Henry, "did de dogs had they supper?"

"They did," said his mamma.

"All de dogs," said his papa.

"Long since," said the nurse woman.

"Well, den," said John Henry, "ain't I as good as de dogs?"

And when John Henry said that he got mad. He reared back in his bed and broke out the slats. He opened his mouth and yowled, and it put out the lamp. He cleaved his tongue and spat, and it put out the fire. "Don't make me mad!" said John Henry, and the thunder rumbled and rolled. "Don't let me git mad on de day I'm bawn, 'cause I'm skeered of my own-se'f when I gits mad."

And John Henry stood up in the middle of the floor and he told them what he wanted to eat. "Bring me four ham bones and a pot full of cabbages," he said. "Bring me a bait of turnip greens tree-top tall, and season hit down wid a side er middlin'. Bring me a pone er cold cawn bread and some hot potlicker to wash hit down. Bring me two hog jowls and a kittleful er whippowill peas. Bring me a skilletful er red-hot biscuits and a big jugful er cane molasses. 'Cause my name is John Henry, and I'll see you soon."

So John Henry walked out of the house and away from the Black River Country where all good rousterbouts are born.

THE BUFFALO SKINNERS

Carl Sandburg called this ballad "the framework of a big, sweeping novel of real life, condensed into a few telling stanzas." Historically, "seventy-three" was the year in which professional

buffalo hunters from Dodge City first came to the Texas Pan-
handle. The Buffalo Skinners can be found in many collections.
This version is from Cowboy Songs and other Frontier Ballads.[1]

Come all you jolly fellows and listen to my song,
There are not many verses, it will not detain you long;
It's concerning some young fellows who did agree to go
And spend one summer pleasantly on the range of the buffalo.

It happened in Jacksboro in the spring of seventy-three,
A man by the name of Crego came stepping up to me,
Saying, "How do you do, young fellow, and how would you
    like to go
And spend one summer pleasantly on the range of the buffalo?"

"It's me being out of employment," this to Crego I did say,
"This going out on the buffalo range depends upon the pay.
But if you will pay good wages and transportation too,
I think, sir, I will go with you to the range of the buffalo."

"Yes, I will pay good wages, give transportation too,
Provided you will go with me and stay the summer through;
But if you should grow homesick, come back to Jacksboro,
I won't pay transportation from the range of the buffalo."

It's now our outfit was complete—seven able-bodied men,
With navy six and needle gun—our troubles did begin;
Our way it was a pleasant one, the route we had to go,
Until we crossed Pease River on the range of the buffalo.

[1]Collected, adapted, and arranged by John A. Lomax and Alan Lomax.
© Copyright 1934 and renewed 1962 Ludlow Music, Inc., New York, N.Y.
Used by permission.

It's now we've crossed Pease River, our troubles have begun.
The first damned tail I went to rip, Christ! how I cut my thumb!
While skinning the damned old stinkers our lives wasn't a
show,
For the Indians watched to pick us off while skinning the
buffalo.

He fed us on such sorry chuck I wished myself most dead,
It was old jerked beef, croton coffee, and sour bread.
Pease River's as salty as hell fire, the water I could never go—
O God! I wished I had never come to the range of the buffalo.

Our meat it was buffalo hump and iron wedge bread,
And all we had to sleep on was a buffalo robe for a bed;
The fleas and gray-backs worked on us, O boys, it was not
slow,
I'll tell you there's no worse hell on earth than the range of
the buffalo.

Our hearts were cased with buffalo hocks, our souls were
cased with steel,
And the hardships of that summer would nearly make us reel.
While skinning the damned old stinkers our lives they had no
show,
For the Indians waited to pick us off on the hills of Mexico.

The season being near over, old Crego he did say
The crowd had been extravagant, was in debt to him that
day—
We coaxed him and we begged him and still it was no go—
We left old Crego's bones to bleach on the range of the
buffalo.

Oh, it's now we've crossed Pease River and homeward we are
  bound,
No more in that hell-fired country shall ever we be found.
Go home to our wives and sweethearts, tell others not to go,
For God's forsaken the buffalo range and the damned old
  buffalo.

THE LANE COUNTY BACHELOR

*This ballad presents the rough side of the American frontier
saga, that of the "loser." Unlike many others who stuck it out
and received full title to their land after farming it for a few
years, Frank Bolar packed up and went home, for reasons
which he makes quite clear in this bitter song. This version
of Bolar's sad account is from Carl Sandburg's* American
Songbag.

My name is Frank Bolar, 'nole bachelor I am,
I'm keepin' ole bach on an elegant plan.
You'll find me out West in the County of Lane
Starving to death on a government claim;
My house is built of the national soil,
The walls are erected according to Hoyle,
The roof has no pitch but is level and plain
And I always get wet when it happens to rain.

Chorus:
        But hurrah for Lane County, the land of the free,
        The home of the grasshopper, bedbug, and flea,
        I'll sing loud her praises and boast of her fame
        While starving to death on my government claim.

My clothes they are ragged, my language is rough,
My head is case-hardened, both solid and tough;
The dough it is scattered all over the room
And the floor would get scared at the sight of a broom;
My dishes are dirty and some in the bed
Covered with sorghum and government bread;
But I have a good time, and live at my ease
On common sop-sorghum, old bacon and grease.

Chorus:

> But hurrah for Lane County, the land of the West,
> Where the farmers and laborers are always at rest,
> Where you've nothing to do but sweetly remain,
> And starve like a man on your government claim.

How happy am I when I crawl into bed,
And a rattlesnake rattles his tail at my head,
And the gay little centipede, void of all fear
Crawls over my pillow and into my ear,
And the nice little bedbug so cheerful and bright,
Keeps me a-scratching full half of the night,
And the gay little flea with toes sharp as a tack
Plays "Why don't you catch me?" all over my back.

Chorus:

> But hurrah for Lane County, where blizzards arise,
> Where the winds never cease and the flea never dies,
> Where the sun is so hot if in it you remain
> 'Twill burn you quite black on your government claim.

How happy am I on my government claim,
Where I've nothing to lose and nothing to gain,
Nothing to eat and nothing to wear,
Nothing from nothing is honest and square.

But here I am stuck, and here I must stay,
My money's all gone and I can't get away;
There's nothing will make a man hard and profane
Like starving to death on a government claim.

Chorus:

> Then come to Lane County, there's room for you all,
> Where the winds never cease and the rains never fall,
> Come join in the chorus and boast of her fame,
> While starving to death on your government claim.

Now don't get discouraged, ye poor hungry men,
We're all here as free as a pig in a pen;
Just stick to your homestead and battle your fleas,
And pray to your Maker to send you a breeze.
Now a word to claim-holders who are bound for to stay:
You may chew your hard-tack till you're toothless and gray,
But as for me, I'll no longer remain
And starve like a dog on my government claim.

Chorus:

> Farewell to Lane County, farewell to the West,
> I'll travel back East to the girl I love best;
> I'll stop in Missouri and get me a wife,
> And live on corn dodgers the rest of my life.

STACKALEE

*This is an early version of "Stackallee," collected by Onah L.
Spencer. No one knows the historical identity of the original
Stackalee (or Stagollee, as he is known in some versions). More
important is the character portrayed in this folk ballad: cruel,
unrepentant, yet somehow appealing.*

It was in the year of eighteen hundred and sixty-one
In St. Louis on Market Street where Stackalee was born.
Everybody's talkin about Stackalee.
It was on one cold and frosty night
When Stackalee and Billy Lyons had one awful fight,
Stackalee got his gun. Boy, he got it fast!
He shot poor Billy through and through;
Bullet broke a lookin glass.
Lord, O Lord, O Lord!
Stackalee shot Billy once; his body fell to the floor.
He cried out, Oh, please Stack, please don't shoot me no more.

The White Elephant Barrel House was wrecked that night;
Gutters full of beer and whiskey; it was an awful sight.
Jewelry and rings of the purest solid gold
Scattered over the dance and gamblin hall.
The can-can dancers they rushed for the door
When Billy cried, Oh, please, Stack, don't shoot me no more.
Have mercy, Billy groaned, Oh, please spare my life;

Stack says, God bless your children, damn your wife!
You stold my magic Stetson; I'm gonna steal your life.
But, says Billy, I always treated you like a man.
'Tain't nothin to that old Stetson but the greasy band.
He shot poor Billy once, he shot him twice,
And the third time Billy pleaded, please go tell my wife.
Yes, Stackalee, the gambler, everybody knowed his name;
Made his livin hollerin high, low, jack and the game.

Meantime the sergeant strapped on his big forty-five,
Says now we'll bring in this bad man, dead or alive.
And brass-buttoned policemen tall dressed in blue
Came down the sidewalk marchin two by two.
Sent for the wagon and it hurried and come
Loaded with pistols and a big gatlin gun.

At midnight on that stormy night there came an awful wail
Billy Lyons and a graveyard ghost outside the city jail.
Jailer, jailer, says Stack, I can't sleep,
For around my bedside poor Billy Lyons still creeps.
He comes in shape of a lion with a blue steel in his hand,
For he knows I'll stand and fight if he comes in the shape of
    man.
Stackalee went to sleep that night by the city clock bell,
Dreaming the devil had come all the way up from hell.
Red devil was sayin, you better hunt your hole;
I've hurried here from hell just to get your soul.

Stackalee told him yes, maybe you're right,
But I'll give even you one hell of a fight.
When they got into the scuffle, I heard the devil shout,
Come and get this bad man before he puts my fire out.
The next time I seed the devil he was scramblin up the wall,
Yellin, come and get this bad man fore he mops up with us all.

II

Then here come Stack's woman runnin, says daddy, I love you
    true;
See what beer, whiskey, and smokin hop has brought you to.
But before I'll let you lay in there, I'll put my life in pawn.
She hurried and got Stackalee out on a five thousand dollar
    bond.
Stackalee said, ain't but one thing that grieves my mind,
When they take me away, babe, I leave you behind.
But the woman he really loved was a voodoo queen
From Creole French market, way down in New Orleans.

He laid down at home that night, took a good night's rest,
Arrived in court at nine o'clock to hear the coroner's inquest.

Crowds jammed the sidewalk, far as you could see,
Tryin to get a good look at tough Stackalee.
Over the cold, dead body Stackalee he did bend,
Then he turned and faced those twelve jury men.
The judge says, Stackalee, I would spare your life,
But I know you're a bad man; I can see it in your red eyes.
The jury heard the witnesses, and they didn't say no more;
They crowded into the jury room, and the messenger closed
    the door.

The jury came to agreement, the clerk he wrote it down,
And everybody was whisperin' he's penitentiary bound.
When the jury walked out, Stackalee didn't budge,
They wrapped the verdic and passed it to the judge.
Judge looked over his glasses, says, Mr. Bad Man Stackalee,
The jury finds you guilty of murder in the first degree.
Now the trail's come to an end, how the folks gave cheers;
Bad Stackalee was sent down to Jefferson pen for seventy-five
    years.

Now late at night you can hear him in his cell,
Arguin with the devil to keep from goin to hell.
And the other convicts whisper, whatcha know about that?
Gonna burn in hell forever over an old Stetson hat!
Everybody's talkin bout Stackalee.
That bad man, Stackalee!

Negro Spirituals

Negro spirituals, which date back to the days of slavery, developed out of a need for an emotional religion to replace the lost African deities. As folklorist Alan Lomax puts it, "The slaves, impressed by the power of the white man's god and feeling the need for some fixed point in a situation deprived of most human values, embraced the faith of their Protestant masters and became ardent Baptists and Methodists."

MOTHERLESS CHILD

Sometimes I feel like a motherless child,
Sometimes I feel like a motherless child,
Sometimes I feel like a motherless child,
A long ways from home,
A long ways from home.

Sometimes I feel like I'm almost gone,
Sometimes I feel like I'm almost gone,
Sometimes I feel like I'm almost gone,
A long ways from home,
A long ways from home.

Sometimes I feel like a feather in the air,
Sometimes I feel like a feather in the air,
Sometimes I feel like a feather in the air,
And I spread my wings and I fly,

I spread my wings and I fly.

NOBODY KNOWS THE TROUBLE I'VE SEEN

Oh nobody knows the trouble I've seen,
Nobody knows but Jesus.
Nobody knows the trouble I've seen,
Glory, Hallelujah!

Sometimes I'm up, sometimes I'm down,
Oh, yes, Lord!
Sometimes I'm almost to the ground,
Oh, yes, Lord!
Although you see me going along, so,
Oh, yes, Lord!
I have my troubles here below,
Oh, yes, Lord!

Nobody knows the trouble I've seen,
Nobody knows my sorrow.
Nobody knows the trouble I've seen,
Glory, Hallelujah!

One day when I was walking along,
Oh, yes, Lord!
The elements opened and his love came down,
Oh, yes, Lord!
I never shall forget that day,
Oh, yes, Lord!
When Jesus washed my sins away,
Oh, yes, Lord!

Oh, nobody knows the trouble I've seen,
Nobody knows my sorrow.
Nobody knows the trouble I've seen,
Glory, Hallelujah!

JOSHUA FIT DE BATTLE OF JERICHO

Joshua fit de battle of Jericho,
Jericho, Jericho,
Joshua fit de battle of Jericho,
And de walls come tumbling down.

You may talk about yo' king of Gideon
Talk about yo' man of Saul,
Dere's none like good old Joshua
At de battle of Jericho.

Up to de walls of Jericho,
He marched with spear in hand;
"Go blow dem ram horns," Joshua cried,
"Kase de battle am in my hand."

Den de lamb ram sheep horns begin to blow,
Trumpets begin to sound,
Joshua commanded de chillen to shout,
And de walls come tumbling down.

Dat morning,
Joshua fit de battle of Jericho,
Jericho, Jericho,
Joshua fit de battle of Jericho,
And de walls come tumbling down.

HOW "ST. LOUIS BLUES" WAS BORN
by W. C. Handy

"St. Louis Blues" is one of the most famous jazz songs of all time. In this selection, its composer, W. C. Handy (1873-1958), describes its creation. One version of the song follows.

It occurred to me that I could perhaps make more headway in [the] direction [of a popular hit] without the questionable help of my four lively and robust youngsters at home, all bent on using my legs for teeter-boards. The noisy rumpus warmed the heart but it put a crimp in my work. I could feel the blues coming on, and I didn't want to be distracted, so I packed my grip and made my getaway.

I rented a room in the Beale Street section and went to work. Outside, the lights flickered. Chitterling joints were as crowded as the more fashionable resorts like the Iroquois. Piano thumpers tickled the ivories in the saloons to attract customers, furnishing a theme for the prayers at Beale Street Baptist Church and Avery Chapel (Methodist). Scores of powerfully built roustabouts from river boats sauntered along the pavement, elbowing fashionable browns in beautiful gowns. Pimps in boxback coats and undented Stetsons came out to get a breath of early evening air and to welcome the young night. The poolhall crowd grew livelier than they had been during the day. All that contributed to the color and spell of Beale Street mingled outside, but I neither saw nor heard it that night. I had a song to write.

My first decision was that my new song would be another blues, true to the soil and in the tradition of "Memphis Blues." Ragtime, I had decided, was passing out. But this number would go beyond its predecessor and break new ground. I would begin with a down-home ditty fit to go with twanging banjos and yellow shoes. Songs of this sort could become tremendous hits sometimes. On the levees at St. Louis I had heard "Looking for the Bully" sung by the roustabouts, which later was adopted and nationally popularized by May Irwin. I had watched the joy-spreaders rarin' to go when it was played by the bands on the *Gray Eagle,* or the *Spread Eagle.* I wanted such a success, but I was determined that my song would have an important difference. The emotions that it expressed were going to be real. Moreover, it was going to be cut to the native blues pattern.

A flood of memories filled my mind. First, there was the picture I had of myself, broke, unshaven, wanting even a decent meal, and standing before the lighted saloon in St. Louis without a shirt under my frayed coat. There was also from that same period a curious and dramatic little fragment that till now had seemed to have little or no importance. While occupied with my own miseries during that sojourn, I had seen a woman whose pain seemed even greater. She had tried to take the edge off her grief by heavy drinking, but it hadn't worked. Stumbling along the poorly lighted street, she muttered as she walked, "Ma man's got a heart like a rock cast in de sea."

The expression interested me, and I stopped another woman to inquire what she meant. She replied, "Lawd, man, it's hard and gone so far from her she can't reach it." Her language was the same down-home medium that conveyed the laughable woe of lamp-blacked lovers in hundreds of frothy songs, but her plight was much too real to provoke much laughter. My song was taking shape. I had now settled upon the mood.

Another recollection pressed in upon me. It was the memory of that odd gent who called figures for the Kentucky breakdown—the one who everlastingly pitched his tones in the key of *G* and moaned the calls like a presiding elder preaching at a revival meeting. Ah, there was my key—I'd do the song in *G*.

Well, that was the beginning. I was definitely on my way. But when I got started, I found that many other considerations also went into the composition. Ragtime had usually sacrificed melody for an exhilarating syncopation. My aim would be to combine ragtime syncopation with a real melody too. The dancers at Dixie Park had convinced me that there was something racial in their response to this rhythm, and I had used it in a disguised form in the "Memphis Blues." Indeed, the very word "tango," as I know now, was derived from the African "tangana," and signified this same tom-tom beat. This would figure in my introduction, as well as in the middle strain.

In the lyric I decided to use Negro phraseology and dialect. I felt then, as I feel now, that this often implies more than well-chosen English can briefly express. My plot centered around the wail of a lovesick woman for her lost man, but in the telling of it I resorted to the humorous spirit of the by-gone coon songs. I used the folk blues' three-line stanza that created the twelve-measure strain.

The primitive Southern Negro as he sang was sure to bear down on the third and seventh tones of the scale, slurring between major and minor. Whether in the cotton fields of the Delta or on the levee up St. Louis way, it was always the same. Till then, however, I had never heard this slur used by a more sophisticated Negro, or by any white man. I had tried to convey this effect in "Memphis Blues" by introducing flat thirds and sevenths (now called "blue notes") into my song, although its prevailing key was the major; and I carried this device into my new melody as well. I also struck upon the idea of using the dominant seventh as the opening chord of the verse. This was a distinct departure, but as it turned out, it touched the spot.

In the folk blues the singer fills up occasional gaps with words like "Oh, lawdy" or "Oh, baby" and the like. This meant that in writing a melody to be sung in the blues manner one would have to provide gaps or waits. In my composition I decided to embellish the piano and orchestra score at these points. This kind of business is called a "break"; entire books of different "breaks" for a single song can be found on the music counters today, and the breaks become a fertile source of the orchestral improvisation which became the essence of jazz. In the chorus I used plagal chords to give spiritual effects in the harmony. Altogether, I aimed to use all that is characteristic of the Negro from Africa to Alabama. By the time I had done all this heavy thinking and remembering, I figured it was time to get something down on paper, so I wrote, "I hate to see de evenin' sun go down." And if you ever had to sleep on the cobbles down by the river in St. Louis, you'll understand that complaint.

St. Louis had come into the composition in more ways than one before the sun peeped through my window. So when the song was completed, I dedicated the new piece to Mr.

Russell Gardner, the St. Louis man who had liked "Jogo Blues," and I proudly christened it the "St. Louis Blues." The same day on Pee Wee's cigar stand I orchestrated the number and jotted down scores for the men of my band.

The song was off my chest, and secretly I was pleased with it, but I could scarely wait for the public verdict. Blurry-eyed from loss of sleep, I went with the band to the evening's engagement on the Alaskan Roof.

The one-step, maxixe and other dances had been done to the tempo of "Memphis Blues," which the Vernon Castles slowed up to introduce their original dance, the fox-trot. When "St. Louis Blues" was written the tango was the vogue. I tricked the dancers by arranging a tango introduction, breaking abruptly then into a low-down blues. My eyes swept the floor anxiously, then suddenly I saw lightning strike. The dancers seem electrified. Something within them came suddenly to life. An instinct that wanted so much to live, to fling its arms and spread joy, took them by the heels. By this I was convinced that my new song was accepted.

When the evening was over, the band piled into cabs and followed me home to celebrate the birth of the new blues. But Maggie, arms akimbo and rolling pin poised, was waiting for Jiggs at the door. I had been away from home twenty-four hours, burning up worlds of energy to produce a song, but maybe I should have stated where I was going and what I intended to do. Failing to make that clear, I presume, the fault was mine. But it's an awkard thing to announce in advance your intention of composing a song hit between midnight and dawn. The talk more naturally follows the act, and that is what ultimately happened in my case.

The men of the band got a kick out of my domestic drama. But after all, heads are made to be lumped in this funny-paper world—aren't they?

A criticism leveled at the "St. Louis Blues" by the trombonist of our band was that it needed a vamp, a vamp in the prevailing manner, to allow more time for the singer.

"Never. Never!" I exploded.

But the next day a pause mark was placed over the final note in the introduction in order to favor the singer with the required delay, and with that "St. Louis Blues" was completed, born in an age of vamps, September, 1914, without a vamp. Two years had elapsed since I first published "Memphis Blues," five years since I played this first jazz composition using Osborne and the tenor sax that moaned like "a sinner on revival day." Well, they say that life begins at forty—I wouldn't know —but I was forty the year "St. Louis Blues" was composed, and ever since then my life has, in one sense at least, revolved around that composition.

ST. LOUIS BLUES
by W. C. Handy

I hate to see de evenin' sun go down,
Hate to see de evenin' sun go down,
'Cause mah baby, he done lef' dis town.

Feelin' tomorrow lak I feel today,
Feel tomorrow lak I feel today,
I'll pack mah trunk, make mah get-away.

St. Louis woman, wid her diamon' rings,
Pulls dat man roun' by her apron strings.
'Twant for powder an' for store-bought hair,
De man I love would not gone nowhere.

Chorus:
 Got de St. Louis blues, jes as blue as I can be,
 Dat man got a heart lak a rock cast in de sea,
 Or else he wouldn't have gone so far from me.
  [Spoken] Doggoneit!

Been to de Gypsy to get mah fortune tole,
To de Gypsy done got mah fortune tole,
'Cause I'm most wile 'bout mah Jelly-Roll.

Gypsy done tole me, "Don't you wear no black."
Yes, she done tole me, "Don't you wear no black.
Go to St. Louis, you can win him back."

Help me to Cairo, make St. Louis by mahself,
Get to Cairo, find mah ole friend Jeff.
Gwine to pin mahself close to his side.
If I flag his train, I sho can ride.

Chorus:
    I loves dat man lak a schoolboy loves his pie,
    Lak a Kentucky Col'nel loves his mint an' rye.
    I'll love mah baby till de day I die.

You ought to see dat stovepipe brown of mine,
Lak he owns de Di'mon' Joseph line.
He'd make a cross-eyed 'oman go stone blind.

Blacker than midnight, teeth lak flags of truce,
Blackest man in de whole St. Louis.
Blacker de berry, sweeter is de juice.

About a crap game he knows a pow'ful lot,
But when work time comes he's on de dot.
Gwine to ask him for a cold ten spot.
What it takes to git it, he's certainly got.

Chorus:
    A black-headed gal make a freight train jump de track,
    Said a black-headed gal make a freight train jump de track.
    But a long tall gal makes a preacher ball de jack.

Lawd, a blonde-headed woman makes a good man leave de town,
I said blonde-headed woman makes a good man leave de town,
But a red-headed woman makes a boy slap his papa down.

Oh, ashes to ashes and dust to dust,
I said ashes to ashes and dust to dust.
If mah blues don't get you, mah jazzing must.

VI. America Sings

TALKING IT OVER

1. What stereotyped attitudes toward millers and lumberjacks are revealed in "The Miller's Three Sons" and "The Frozen Logger"?

2. Why do you suppose Casey Jones has become so famous, considering that so many engineers have been killed in railroad accidents?

3. a) How is John Henry portrayed as a true folk hero? In what ways does he resemble a mythical demigod like Paul Bunyan?
b) What aspect of John Henry's contest with the steam drill is especially relevant today?

4. What do Young Monroe, John Henry, and Casey Jones, as they are portrayed in this part of the book, have in common?

5. In "The Buffalo Skinners," what was the conflict between the men and their boss, Crego? How was the conflict resolved?

6. What are some of the reasons mentioned by Frank Bolar in "The Lane County Bachelor" for his disillusionment with frontier life? Why do you think many others succeeded where he failed?

7. What songs in this part of the book appear to contain humor? Compare the different kinds of humor employed.

8. Did you find anything appealing about Stackalee, as the song portrays him? Explain.

9. What common characteristics and attitudes do the three Negro spirituals reveal?

SCRIBNER STUDENT PAPERBACKS